IAN FLETCHER
POET AND SCHOLAR

IAN FLETCHER
(1920–1988)
POET AND SCHOLAR:

A LIST OF HIS PUBLICATIONS

A. S. G. Edwards, Peter Mendes and John Stokes

Introduction by John Stokes

All rights reserved. No part of this work covered by the copyright herein may be reproduced or used in any means—graphic, electronic, or mechanical, including copying, recording, taping, or information storage and retrieval systems—without written permission of the publisher.

Printed by imprintdigital
Upton Pyne, Exeter
www.digital.imprint.co.uk

Typesetting by narrator
www.narrator.me.uk
info@narrator.me.uk
033 022 300 39

Published by Shoestring Press
19 Devonshire Avenue, Beeston, Nottingham, NG9 1BS
(0115) 925 1827
www.shoestringpress.co.uk

This limited edition of 300 copies published 2019
© Copyright: A. S. G. Edwards, Peter Mendes and John Stokes
© Cover illustration of Ian Fletcher by Pauline Lucas

The moral rights of the authors have been asserted.

ISBN 978-1-912524-28-0

PREFACE

This memoir and list of publications is a belated tribute of appreciation and affection to our former teacher. We are keenly conscious that the list of his publications is unlikely to be complete. Some have been lost through circumstances beyond our control (there does not appear to be a complete surviving file of the *Tripoli Times*, for instance); others, in little magazines of the 1940s and 1950s, have doubtless been overlooked. Also, we have aimed to record instances where items, in verse or prose, that appeared first in periodicals were subsequently reprinted in books; since some poems may have changed title and/or text, we may have failed to identify some items. But what we have identified displays the contours of a remarkable career, chronicled in John Stokes's memoir.

We are indebted for the kind assistance of the staffs of the London Library; Senate House Library, University of London; Jennifer Glanville, University of Reading, Department of Special Collections; Cambridge University Library and the British Library, and to Robert Weaver of Dulwich College; Dr Elspeth Healey, Special Collections Librarian, Spencer Library, University of Kansas, Lawrence, Kansas; Dr Alison Fraser, Deputy Curator, The Poetry Collection of the University Libraries, University at Buffalo, the State University of New York; Professor J. R. O'Donnell, Librarian, Arizona State University Library, Tempe, Arizona, Katherine Krzys, Curator, Rare Books and Manuscripts, Arizona State University Library. We have benefitted greatly from the professional expertise of Faith Evans and Valerie Mendes. Dr Loraine Fletcher has been exceptionally generous in offering information, materials and support.

The spelling of the Christian name varies between 'Iain' and 'Ian.' We have not consistently differentiated the forms in our record of his writings.

ABBREVIATIONS

*: verse

BPP: Ian Fletcher, ed., *British poetry and prose, 1870-1905* (Oxford: Oxford University Press, 1987)

ELT: *English Literature in Transition, 1880-1920*

MLR: *Modern Language Review*

TLS: *Times Literary Supplement*

WBYC: Ian Fletcher, *W. B. Yeats and his Contemporaries* (Brighton: Harvester, 1987)

INTRODUCTION

Ian Fletcher was both scholar and poet. There's nothing unusual about that, but in Fletcher's case the dividing line was exceptionally fluid because his prose was driven by the same exuberant love of language as his verse. Verbal virtuosity even characterized his correspondence—and some of his most evocative writing was in his letters. He was always the most generous of scholars, eager to share information. Confronted by attitudes he found unsympathetic he could be quite fierce, both in person and on the page, but he lacked the competitiveness that can bedevil academic life and he happily dispensed ideas and encouragement to colleagues, friends, students, to anyone who showed an interest in the things that interested him, across two continents.

Born on 22 August 1920, brought up in South London by his mother, Fletcher attended Dulwich College, leaving in 1936. He later worked as a Children's Librarian for Lewisham Borough Council while enrolled as an Evening Student at Goldsmith's College, University of London. Formal studies were interrupted in 1941 by military service, much of which was spent in the Middle East—in Egypt, Libya, Sudan, Palestine and Syria—where his literary abilities and his poor eyesight, neither appropriate to serious soldiering, became very apparent. Seconded from the army in 1943 he was made Deputy Information Officer and was sub-editor of the *Tripoli Times* from 1944–5 and Staff Writer for the Ministry of Information in Cairo from 1945–6. On his discharge he resumed work as a librarian, completing exams in Local Government. His professional life changed dramatically in 1956 when, in a frequently told story, he was appointed without even an undergraduate degree to a lectureship in the English Department at Reading University. He gained a PhD from Reading in 1965. From the time of his appointment he was a fully functioning academic. Although solidly based at Reading he spent time in North America on various visiting appointments in the 1960s and 1970s. In 1981 he left Reading to take up a Professorship at Arizona State University at Tempe where he taught until taking retirement in

1984. He died in Birmingham on 2 November 1988 from complications following hepatitis contracted in wartime.

Fletcher was the stuff of legend even in his lifetime and there are memorable portraits by people who knew him well in G. S. Fraser's *A Stranger and Afraid* (Manchester: Carcanet New Press, 1983), Derek Stanford's 'Remembering Ian Fletcher' (*London Magazine*, February 1990: 73–80) Frank Kermode's *Not Entitled* (London: HarperCollins, 1996), Peter Porter's introduction to Fletcher's *Collected Poems* (Nottingham: Shoestring Press, 1998, pp. 1–7), John Lucas's *Next Year Will Be Better* (Nottingham: Five Leaves Press, 2010), and, above all, in Loraine Fletcher's detailed personal and literary autobiography, *Print/Capture: A Memoir* (The Female Quixote Press, Kindle Edition, 2013). Fraser, who was also in Egypt, describes him in those days as 'a young poet with short-sighted angry eyes, a comic snub nose, and a mouth that twisted eloquently in disgust and sorrow' (p. 166). But it's his voice that colleagues and students still hear when they remember their university days in Reading or, no doubt, in Illinois or Arizona. It was amazingly loud, and he was amazingly loquacious. The vocal sounds he could make ranged from a peremptory bark to a lofty elocutionary tone—useful in the lecture hall but by no means confined to it—to a kind of clerical intoning he adopted when he recited poetry, often just to himself. When amused, which was often, he chortled with unique vigour. Frank Kermode recalls him 'roaring and booming' around the Reading English Department (p. 88); John Lucas says that his voice had 'greater range and volume than any other voice I have known' (p. 239). Anyone who heard him would surely say the same.

It would be easy to assume from voice alone that Fletcher was a scion of the English upper-middle class, but, in fact, the family background was distantly Scottish—a fact of which he was proud, hence his early adoption of the 'Iain' spelling —and his upbringing was suburban. In a comparatively rare reference to his childhood, made in 1950, he writes (*Poetry Review*, 41 (1950), 156):

> William Morris was the first poet whom I read seriously, being fourteen. *The Defence of Guenevere* still moves my mind, not to an excitement, but to a kind of midnight

trance, when I am content to serve at a Christmas Mystery with Galahad, or feel the silent sonority of King Arthur's Tomb between those two lovers, his Queen and knight.

An ability to recreate and participate in fictional scenes is common among imaginative children, especially when they have no siblings, but the solemnity that Fletcher records here—the 'midnight trance'—is striking. A combination of the sacred and the proto-erotic—the 'two lovers'—suggests romantic identifications that were to develop and deepen in his youth, helped by a familiarity with classical literature, with literature of every kind in fact, including military history, and—even more unusual for an adolescent—with theology.

As this bibliography makes very clear, Fletcher wrote throughout his life. There were few fallow periods, even when he was in poor health or heavily committed to teaching, no genre that he wouldn't take on. Writer's block seems to have been unknown to him and there were always new projects underway, though several, too many, went unfulfilled or unpublished— including, it's said, at least one novel, probably scurrilous. Otherwise, nothing but 'scribble, scribble' as he would sometimes complain about himself. His vocabulary was bottomless; the possibilities of outrageous formulations without end. In the Introduction to *British Fiction 1880—1900* (Oxford, 1972) he preempted criticism at having failed to provide representativeness with the apologia: 'the reader will soon enough divine the direction of my taste: the florid, the bizarre, the extreme, the unread. I hope, nonetheless, that I communicate by my selections some relish for the plain style, for irony, and for the insight of historical and social interest.'

In his own writing, however, 'the plain style' was impossible to maintain, whatever the subject. Words sprout in multiple combinations ('taut stoicism', 'acridly spiced', 'painful limpidity,' 'smokily eloquent factories') and technical terms that would otherwise rarely leave handbooks of rhetoric such as 'paronomasia', 'technopaegnia' and 'epizeuxis' flourish in the overheated environment. There are words that journey from their philosophical origin to serve a more existential function:

'hypostasis', 'anamorphosis', for instance, which are redeployed to invoke states of being. The style—'baroque', 'rococo', however one terms it—was both entirely personal and consciously antiquated. Lexical skill was, on one level, simply what writing was about, with the result that, though never dull, even in print Fletcher could be rather noisy, carried away by sound alone.

One of the other great rewards of the bibliography is that it suggests—without actually dissolving the mystery of Fletcher's learning—a variety of cultural contexts and reveals shifts of attention as well as continuities in the development of a unique literary personality. Fletcher's breadth of reading is revealed in the number of translations he published, even when quite young, and the number of languages he could negotiate. There are translations from Latin, Greek, French, even Portuguese (but, tellingly perhaps, no German). Presumably Dulwich College, though it may not have made much impression on him academically, did manage to supply a basic grounding in the classics. It certainly didn't inhibit an ambitious young poet. The College Archives contain an exercise book dated 1935: 'SELECTED POEMS by I. FLETCHER.' Hand-written, but set out like a proper book, this has more than fifty poems and is accompanied by a note addressed to 'W. A. M. Leake Esq' (Head of Dulwich College Preparatory School).

> Dear Sir, I have enclosed, or rather left several sheets at the back of the Book for Criticism. And if you have any destructive criticism to make, sir, will you please put it at back with title of poem, just mentioning the line.
> I am yrs.
> Very sincerely
> Ian Fletcher

Many adolescents write up their lives portentously (and sometimes morbidly), anticipating what is to come; few have Fletcher's sense of vocation. There are squibs mocking his contemporaries (this was to become a lifelong habit), but overall it's the sonnet form that predominates, with hints of Yeats and of Rossetti among others. There are portions of plays (from

Nocturnal Glamour, subtitled 'a comedy', *Lucretius*, 'a tragedy', and *Alfred*, 'first play in *Steps to Destiny*'). There's a poem reimagining the battle of Sedgmoor in 1685, final surge of the Monmouth rebellion against James II, which anticipates the mature writer's penchant for historical subjects as well as for elegy. It ends, with haphazard punctuation:

> Sometimes, at the dead of night,
> When fog, swirls o'er the moor, in living waves
> They, fight it again, that glorious fight
> And Soldiers spring, from Gory, Graves.

Death is a major preoccupation throughout (again not uncommon among the young), provoked in more than one case by the ambiguous shadows still cast by the First War. A poem entitled 'AUGUST 4th, 1914.' is unexpectedly infused with Pre-Raphaelite chivalry:

> When war came, I went… and girded
> On my ember robe of solitude
> And on my way, came to a church
> Ivey [*sic*] covered and grey, and entered
> And there breathed on me, quiet serene
> Eternal truth flashed upon me
> This is the beginning of the End
> And So! My soul caught a pale glimpse
> Of the Work to come: And I was silent
> And turned and left the place of worship
> With heart, so strangely mingled with
> Joy and sorrow. Nor could I express
> My true emotion. But now, I know, t'was gladness.

By comparison with the Dulwich experience, the time spent at Goldsmith's College was clearly intellectually formative, though few records remain of what sounds like a remarkable educational experiment. Fletcher was particularly impressed by two lecturers: A. E. Douglas-Smith, an educationalist who went on to work for Cambridge's extra-mural programme, and Hermann Peschmann, who was more deeply concerned with poetry. Both men were involved with the student magazine *The Anvil* and contributed ominous editorials. Douglas-Smith in *The Anvil*, 2 (1937), 135 wrote

> These are anxious days; no-one can clearly see very far ahead in the gloom of European politics... one and all, the nations are flocking to age-old panaceas—a belief that if might is not right it is at least a very effective and well-nigh unanswerable substitute for it. Physical culture is receiving in this country a degree of official Government support it has never enjoyed before; and this is very good, even if some of us feel it is the right thing for the wrong reason. But another, wholly bad thing, too, grows so easily in days of anxiety—a hasty and unbalanced conception of the real issues at stake. And that is where institutes such as ours have so important a part to play, offering a liberal evening education closely akin to that of a University, whose purpose is, according to Newman, to cultivate in man or woman a trained judgment, and the power, quickly and unerringly, to choose the better and reject the worse.

Fletcher contributed poems to *The Anvil* and (not for the last time) helped draw up a cricket team. He would certainly have attended Peschmann's lectures, information about which is in the Evening Department Adult Education Prospectuses 1937–1938 and 1938–1939, in Special Collections, Goldsmith's College. These included 'The Romantic Element in English Literature' (from Tennyson, Browning etc to Walter de la Mare and 'Mr. W. B. Yeats') and 'Poetry of Today': 'ranging from patriotic idealism (Rupert Brooke) to bitterness (Siegfried Sassoon), or pity (Wilfred Owen), through the esoteric escapism of Pound and the Sitwells, and the license of Lawrence to the apotheosis of despair, The Waste Land ... Meanwhile, there stands apart the lonely figure of W. B. Yeats, greatest of contemporary poets.' The course description concludes with the no doubt welcome news that 'The writing of original verse is actively encouraged.' Peschmann also taught a course on 'Poetry in the Modern World', which meant in effect since the Great War as 'the reverberations of that conflict have not yet ceased, and it is in our poetry—literature's most sensitive instrument—that they are, perhaps, most sensitively recorded.'

Throughout his career—he went on writing criticism until the 1970s—Peschmann advocated a set of aesthetic principles based on a fundamental distinction between art, with its 'sensitivity', and 'propaganda.' The introduction to *The Voice of Poetry (1930–1950)*, (London: Evans Brothers, 1950), an anthology he edited (which included a poem by Fletcher) still insists that when the one is at the mercy of the other a process of 'enslavement' takes place (p. xxvii).

Leaving Goldsmith's without a formal qualification, Fletcher found himself in the army—and in North Africa. Here, by his own admission, he had time on his hands and he amused himself and others by composing lengthy verse satires, sometimes directed at colleagues, sometimes at major political figures. Locally produced from typescript, these astonishing tirades, which have never been reprinted, are alternately scabrous and deeply felt, products of a sensibility driven to comic distraction by circumstance, by an irrepressible instinct to make verse, and by a mind already crowded with literature. They tell us more about daily life—its frustrations and its outlets—in the armed forces than many more obviously heroic narratives. Fletcher's epics are mock—and all the better for it.

A Satire on the Rise of Learning in the Dark Sudan is dated 'Khartoum 21/10/42—27/11/42' and it features a convocation of fellow soldiers, presided over by a 'Bishop', obviously drunk, who judges them as sinners according to their religious or political affiliations. They include John Day (Buddhist), Kenneth Rowe (Pessimist and Hemingway fan), Gittings (Religionist), Obadiah Banks (Salvationist), Stevens (snobbish, social climbing 'Egoist'), Beckett (Positivist), Callen (Hedonist) and Bert Storey (Communist). In each case individual flaws are itemised by the satirist. So, for instance, Stevens is a tedious nature-lover, always a Fletcher *bête noire*:

> 'Look, Fletcher, here are flowers red white and blue,
> And sometimes pink and pansy-featured too,
> In noble but unpunctuated verse

> Let us their floral fragrancy rehearse.'
> But Fletcher over toadstools grows more crazy
> And turns aside to piss upon a daisy.

Nonetheless, 'Fletcher' reserves his cruellest judgment for himself, in the shape of 'a shambling poet, green eyes and snubby nose/ With sodden fungi sniggering 'tween his toes' who is driven by his own demons.

> An inward malice vaguely to evince
> In furtive nuances and snickering hints
> The pompous words devouring night and day,
> Each qualified comme ça, 'That is to say',
> 'By this I mean' or 'In effect'
> 'I.e.' 'q.v.—I gurgle and dissect,
> I am The Critic; I stand, dirty, aloof,
> My hoarse discourses lifting off the roof.
> I am The Poet, and no one has a gleaning
> Of any tiny line's most tiny meaning.

At the poem's culmination, an obvious recall of its eighteenth-century models, Pope's *Dunciad* in particular, 'Frenzy re-assumes her rabid reign.'

The Principle of Perversion & Disgrace. Testament of my Political Man, some 500 lines long, is dated 'Sept. 1942–March 17 1943', and dedicated (somewhat puzzlingly, though pacifism was probably the point) 'To the insipid homosexuals of Cambridge.' On this occasion the poet reviews pre-war politics with considerable animus, though his over-arching concern claims to be the relation of Church to State. No one escapes witticism: neither Laval ('that orang-utan Pierre Laval reveals the Facist [*sic*] Fang'), nor Mussolini ('pot-bellied Musso knocks down Abbysinia), nor, of course, Hitler himself ('Adolf leers at Polish-built Gdynia'). At home it's almost as bad. Stanley Baldwin 'hangs around the Universities like a loafer | using the House of Commons as a sofa.' Lord Halifax is 'A shambling ape, a clerical buffoon, | who drawls and stutters through his silver spoon; | like whisky-baron's cocktail shaker, | a half-baked Facist [*sic*], dressed like an undertaker, | he goes about, embarrassing his maker.' Worst of all there's the 'scrofulous Chamberlain' who 'gave the Fascists time to rape and whore | And would no doubt have loved to give them more. | Who after Dunkirk would have sought release | In bilious havens of negotiated peace!' These individual attacks follow on from a generalized history of England and, inter alia, a splenetic (and perhaps personally weighted) attack on the political inheritance of public schools as 'a twisted institution for long-perpetuated social prostitution', together with a contemptuous dismissal of imperial power as the unholy result of business greed coupled with puritan zeal.

There's not much confidence in any post-war future either. The envisaged victory—when 'Churchill saunters in der Führer's room'—will be Pyrrhic at most. The prospect of a cleansing colonial revolt is unlikely:

> I can't see Freedom anywhere in sight:
> Jamaica's negros might perhaps confirm
> this tiny sermon on the bourgeois worm.
> Supremest India awaits her fate
> while the squat sinners fumble at the gate.
> Old, transcendental Ghandi's all to blame
> his babbling plays the Britisher's own game:
> another hundred years perhaps may see
> India at last, consummate, clean and free
> With the last Englishman kicked out to sea!

The Principle of Perversion & Disgrace is a prodigious *tour de force* that trumps its Augustan models with some Audenesque tricks. Compact syllepses revisit a dreary inter-war world of passive commuters.

> After the nibbling four years war
> t'establish an England worth fighting for
> the lost and uncompunctive generation threw
> overboard such dreams, a hostile type of crew
> and wriggled back to pub and then to pew.
> The little job in the gasworks would supply
> After demobbing, enough to live and die.
> Après moi, the hot and heavy rains,
> but for today the smug suburban trains.

At the poem's summation, trust in a Church, which should be the 'organized responsibility of man | toward God, established in a human plan', is overwhelmed: 'Both Church and State in tatters shall decay | And glorious Anarchy shall pave the way.'

Despite that, the poet remained true, on occasion, to his devotions. *A Passion Play* (1943) is conventional, inspired by medieval drama, an exercise in biblical reconstruction following the examples of Eliot and Christopher Fry. Yet Satan's speeches have a genuinely gothic, Fletcherian ring to them:

> The temple veil is split in twain and the forests moan
> like the anger of many dragons. This is the time when all
> my servants have power; when the vampire oozes from
> the grave like marsh-mist, and the were-wolf worries the
> child's skull. In a hundred fields the obscure incense
> swirls. The old gods have come back. From the swamp
> and the forests, from the mouldering gable, from the
> dangerous arch, they come with toothless cries, with
> senile excitement, to celebrate sin and death. Now God
> has died His death, and Love is dead. (p. 33)

As G. S. Fraser records, among his contemporaries Fletcher's enthusiasm for theology was unique, although even at this early stage its appeal was probably as a branch of philosophy and a source of poetry rather than as a system of belief. Nor does the theological preoccupation seem quite so strange when one remembers that Kierkegaard, for instance, was of interest to many post-war existentialists. *An Epistle to Kenneth Topley Esq.* (Fraser in *A Stranger and Afraid*, 166, describes Topley as 'a blunt young RAF officer, an ineffectual hearty'), published privately in Tripoli in 1945 is made up of yet more couplets, and as it moves from religion and philosophy (with suggestions of Dryden) to sexuality it shows that Fletcher was very much aware of contemporary intellectual currents even if he was unwilling to swim in them:

> The Humanists will get you, if you wait.
> Broad is the path, and massive is the gate.
> Avid for all, but to no doctrine tied,

> Fortuitously allied and disallied,
> Not knowing what exactly to decide
> Not to decide. A vile eristic crew.
> O leave them to rejoice their musty stew.
> Roccoco [*sic*] echeleons or angels bear
> Our intellectual canopy elsewhere....
>
> Redeem the suture of the *Freudian* gash
> Dilute the sullen *Existential* hash
> Restrain my errings in the shops of Marx,
> Disqualify my *Acquinatic* larks:
> Give me the art of off the record verse.
> Like George, without a too mimetic curse ...
>
> The old desire for the womb's cosmology
> Sailing to an immanence of nothing on a defunctive sea.
> So here's good end, my narcissistic paean.
> I am, dear Kenneth, yours entirely, *Iain*. (pp. 7–8)

In North Africa Fletcher had found himself among a small circle of aspiring *littérateurs*, would-be professionals, as well as by men who took to writing verse only for the duration of the war. There wasn't much else to do. As an editor on the *Tripoli Times* he was able to publish his thoughts on writers as diverse as Scott Fitzgerald, Ezra Pound and Joseph Conrad, and to indulge his own taste for moody topography. Looking back much later, Fletcher distinguished the experience that he and his friends endured from what was going on elsewhere. 'If there was boredom on the Western Front, it was punctuated for the most part by danger', he acknowledged in *Return to Oasis: War Poems and Recollections from the Middle East 1940–1946* (London: Shepheard-Walwyn, 1980): 'Boredom, sand and flies made up much of my own personal experience in the Middle East' (p. xxix). He had confessed as much in a series of pungent vignettes in this collection; in 'Unquiet Lives at the Base' (p. 90):

> The soldiers whose heroic vacancy appals:
> The flaccid cigarette that crowns the face;
> The moon-blank eyes in sicksweet urinals.

or, via a persona, 'Trooper Tufty Trotwell' (p. 90):

> That girl with the egg-curved face and the serpent lips
> will only ask Americans to cough:
> in spite of my ginger moustache, my
> money is not coloured enough.

Fletcher's fondness for bawdy was, of course, shared with other soldier poets and, as with those others, his disrespectful treatment of military service can be heard as a ribald response to the official, Churchillian, oratory of the time and, perhaps, as a refusal to submit too promptly to its calls to duty. Yet the sheer fecundity of Fletcher's language sets him apart, as in 'Soldiers at the Base' (p. 157):

> So I, raw poet, notionally quite least
> Of such uncompassed travellers, come
> By war, all langour, on this middling east
> And jeopard in survival's trivium.

Who else would have deployed the verb 'jeopard' ('to put at risk') and coupled it with 'trivium' ('an introductory course at a medieval university involving the study of grammar, rhetoric, and logic')?

In 1944 Fletcher delivered a lecture at the Sudan Cultural Centre on 'The Relationship Between Literature and Propaganda', the substance of which was later printed, under this title, in *Poetry London*, 2 (1944), 208–12. The lecture begins with an attempt to define the 'Nature of Art':

> The raw material of the Artist is his experience. At the
> present time, when his experiences are liable to be more
> 'shrill,' shall we say, than is usual, there is a tendency
> towards losing that sense of values which is
> indispensable to good art. This tempts the artist into not
> following the faithful road of his own experience, his
> immediate feelings, but writing down what a liberal
> education may point to as fitting for the occasion.

The artist is therefore to be distinguished from the 'man in the street', the 'average man', by virtue of his absolute independence.

> The Artist is not, as Plato thought, a frenzied animal; you will remember the passage in one of his minor dialogues where Socrates points out to Ion that when making his commentaries on Homer he is not aware of the meaning of his words; and it is only afterwards, when his experience of procreating Art is ended, that he is able no longer to identify himself with what he has written, but to stand aside and contemplate it as he would any other thing, that he understands.
> Nor, again, can I agree with the Freudians who say that the Artist is a man who is 'out of Joint with Society', that he is a man who is unable to come to terms with life, and that his art is a compensation-mechanism; so that by means of expressing the common experiences and sufferings of the community he lives in, he is reintegrated with that community.
> No, the Artist is neither mystic nor invalid. He is as healthy as the next man ...

Then, via Milton, the gospels, Stephen Spender, the Spanish Civil War, to land on Coleridge:

> But Art is not action itself, nor is it a negative as suffering is. The action of Art is confined strictly to its own limits. The Artist may be a political animal, or a soldier, but his understanding of life, his coming to terms with life, political or military, is only a means to an end. His end is unique. It is Art, the best words in the best order.

The underlying contrast here is between 'propaganda'—which narrowly prioritises action—and Art whose 'essence ... is elusiveness.' It was Peschmann's distinction refashioned. Fletcher's own commitment to freedom of expression was to remain with him for the rest of his life; more immediately it was put to work in the world of little magazines, of public readings, Third Programme broadcasts, the *causerie* of postwar literary London. Although he is too idiosyncratic to be placed within any movement, however loose, he does share characteristics with his contemporaries and he appears, as poet and reviewer, in the little magazines of the period such as *Nine* and his own periodical *Colonnade*, alongside many writers whose names have more or less survived—David Gascoyne, George Barker, Dylan Thomas, Lawrence Durrell, Nicholas Moore, John Heath Stubbs, Kathleen Raine, Anne Ridler, Michael Hamburger, Muriel Spark, F. T. Prince. Even during the war years he had contributed to *New Vision*, a radical, anti-imperialist publication dedicated to progressive ideals. It might even be tempting to put him in among the neo-Christians—were it not for the bawdy, the conspicuous breadth of learning, the predominance of form, and the refusal to maintain a straight face and tone of voice for very long at all.

The 1940s also saw him broaden his expertise in the visual arts and architecture. (As the art historian Simon Wilson once remarked, in later life 'he could have walked into the Courtauld any time and held his own'). He even made some forays into the theatre. In April 1948 'The Unrecognised Theatre Company' presented a new comedy written by Fletcher in collaboration with Peter Myers (who went on to compose lyrics for revues and musicals) and entitled *Get Up What Stairs?* at the tiny Torch Theatre in Knightsbridge. 'The difficulty of housing a dozen or more people in a pre-fabricated bungalow seems to be the basis of this very erratic farce', as reported in *The Stage*, 20 May 1948:

> Comments on current politics and local councils, the eccentricities of a large family, precocious children, and a crooked councillor are also introduced. A good deal of hearty effort is put into the acting and production, and the work of Mr. Myers and Mr. Fletcher undoubtedly has sincerity of intention and zest.

Unfortunately, this was not enough; the report goes on: 'the whole is just unfunny. We wait in vain for the tricks of technique of the imagination or invention that might turn the stale and stunted into something lively and amusing.'

In 1949 Fletcher's liturgical drama *A Passion Play*, written and published in North Africa, was presented at St. Thomas's church in Regent Street with music by John Buckland. Thanks to Eliot and Fry, along with Charles Williams and Ronald Duncan, poetic plays on biblical themes were in vogue. *The Stage* again records, on 7 April 1949:

> Advantage was taken of the opportunities for dramatic acting in this, the most moving drama of all time. Light and shade were introduced in the poignant contrast between the white purity of Gabriel and the red and black villainy of Satan, and between the dark fear of man and the love of God. Ironic pathos was painted on with a thick brush when the stricken world pleaded for a saviour and then did not recognise Him when He came, but rather wished to destroy.

Intriguingly, Fletcher himself seems to have taken part—no doubt putting that voice to impressive use.

Reviews written around this time and into the 1960s show that Fletcher's interest in the seventeenth century accompanied and even preceded his fascination with the *fin de siècle*. There are obvious similarities. Both eras pursue the links between sex and death down some dark corridors. It was possible to write in defence of Rochester, for instance, in much the same way as one wrote about Ernest Dowson or Lionel Johnson. Similarly, the power of 'the image', common to both periods, connects emblem books with late nineteenth-century symbolism. A review of George Woodcock's book on Aphra Behn in *Poetry Review*, 40 (1949), 61 (long before her revival) identifies her as a prototypical 'New Woman.'

Nevertheless, it was soon becoming clear that Fletcher's greatest contribution would be the recovery of ancient aesthetes and delinquent decadents. The long-established fascination with theology would bolster his scholarly expertise when dealing with the more arcane reading of Pater, Wilde, Symons and Yeats. And the earlier insistence upon the special status of art in a politicized world, its distance from 'propaganda', would provide a basis from which to develop his own style of aestheticism, inspired by exemplary artist-antiheroes for whom art was self-evidently superior to 'primitive' nature. Aubrey Beardsley, in a spectacular paragraph in his book of this title (1987, p. 183) is said to have

> ... decomposed the materials of the objective world and recomposed them into an ideal geography of his own devisal. And all this was accomplished with an icy fire of consciousness, a cold intensity that appears at first antithetical to the sensational, even melodramatic, features of much of his art, and to the frenetic quest for all that can be clutched and held and possessed by one who was continuously in a state of physical dissolution.

Sex and religion, overshadowed by death, meet in a kind of ecstasy, but not without difficulty. The guilt-ridden Arthur Symons, for instance, 'still invested religious language with an emotional significance that was largely factitious. Still chained to Christian culture, he had no other language when he wished to move beyond the merely "visible world", though he was to experiment rather tepidly ... Symons wishes not merely to invert the sacred and the profane, but also to make sexuality a substitute for lost numinousness' (*BPP*, xxii–xxiii). The failure of decadence entirely to replace religious belief with momentary erotic pleasure merely adds to its pathos. After all, 'decadent religiosity is no more than an attempt at sublimating loneliness' (*BPP*, xlviii).

Fletcher's own post-war poetry often takes 'loneliness', distance, as one of its major subjects. A good example of what G. S. Fraser called his 'neo-metaphysical' style is 'Time and Motion Study' which appeared in 1956 in Fraser's anthology *Poetry Now: An Anthology* (London: Faber & Faber, 1956) pp. 63–64. Apparently inspired by contemporary science, its address to the stars depends upon a macrocosmic conceit:

> What are they? Why, only qualities of light
> That once or twice were fractured into form:
> Short wisps or rags that sting the touch or sight,
> Dancing in famine through a night of storm:

> Cold images of heat corrupt within
> Whose mercies rattle in a bowl of tin.

The poem then proceeds over eight stanzas with an amalgam of Christian and classical references only to end with a kind of temporal agnosticism:

> How should I ask for witnesses to speak,
> Tethered in graves, watchmen who never saw,
> But in their majesty of distance gave
> Me mandate to believe these sighs might save.

We can still hear some Eliot in this ('my life is always moved, but always still') some Yeats ('cold images'); Frances Thompson's 'The Hound of Heaven' and even Gerard Manley Hopkins may also play their part. The most persistent echo, though, is of Lionel Johnson whose *Collected Poems* Fletcher had edited in 1953 and about whom he wrote a pioneering essay in 1955. Lines like these:

> What I would do, I do not, doing
> All that I hate; pursued, myself pursuing.

Paradoxically the poem is authentically Fletcherian by virtue of its complex derivations, its vatic gestures and its formal ingenuity. In 'A Villanelle at the Black and White Milk Bar' (*Collected Poems*, 91) we see the particularly demanding constraints of the 'villanelle' form, quite commonly revived in the late nineteenth century, and again in the 1930s by William Empson. Here a yearningly incompetent male faces up to a contemporary *femme fatale* in dispiriting circumstances.

> In milk-bars when the green and curdled light
> Is poured like some emulsion from the walls,
> The warm derisive beauty fades from sight.
>
> He flinched from her face in cheap dance halls;
> She makes a mocking sacrament of flight;
> While the dry beauty of the shadow falls.

The memories are unsatisfactory and the would-be lover turns back into himself.

> And now and always these memorials
> Crumble between his fingers being slight:
> The warm derisive beauty fades from sight.
> The dry beauty of the shadow falls.

Similar effects are achieved in 'Young girls in flower at the youth centre' (*Collected Poems*, 100–101), where the first part observes teenagers, while the second switches to—of all things—the Egyptian fertility god known as 'Ea', and the third part counsels sexual as well as 'metaphysical' resignation:

> The cosmic and the sexual are at one:
> Donzelle shrouded in a maiden dew,
> These verses teach whose shadow you must shun,
> Whose lurid hungers overshadow you.

Equally *recherché* in their way, yet frankly contemporary, are the handful of fine poems about church architecture collected in *Motets* (1962). Confronted with ecclesiastical decay Philip Larkin slipped on his cycle-clips and took his leave; Fletcher lingers to ruminate and to relish the remnants. The wooden cupids that adorn a baroque organ in 'a northern church':

> Now like the natural shapes we find in caves,
> Born sadly from great fractures of the world,
> And formed as water and as rock behaves,
> Where downward groping arches pierce old graves,
> They wait in smothered light with bat wings furled.
> (*Collected Poems*, 78)

As a critic, he had turned increasingly to a fellow apostate, Walter Pater, about whom he wrote a short book still unmatched for its empathic understanding of this shy, self-absorbed, but intellectually determined writer. Pater, again paradoxically, allowed Fletcher to be magisterial on his own terms and in his own way. 'As I have Walter Pater for master,' he announced late on, 'I make no pretence of grading poems in relation to poems by other poets. And if I happen not to like something, I do not write about it' (*WBYC*, p. 338). True enough; it had always been the case.

Securely employed at Reading, at ease in academic circles, working alongside Frank Kermode and Donald Gordon, Head of the English Department, a distinguished Renaissance scholar strongly influenced by the methods of the Warburg Institute, he produced in the late 1950s a number of essays, closely connected with Pater, that have become classics of their kind. Among the most telling, because it serves as summation of his ideas up until that point, is a talk entitled *'Leda and St Anne'*, first delivered on the Third Programme and then printed in *The Listener*, 21 February, 1957, 305–07. It starts with Yeats's decision to print Pater's celebrated passage on the Mona Lisa in *The Oxford Book of Modern Verse* (1936). Yeats's own explanation for this unusual move is described by Fletcher, in a characteristic phrase, as 'richly obscure'—which doesn't stop him from providing his own brilliant rationale. The Mona Lisa passage 'is in a sense, the first modern poem; it grasps an aspect of reality, a convergence of forces, by a quite other method than that of discursive reason' which leads, in turn, to mention of related figures from the 1890s—the Sphinx, Salome and so on—before shifting to Eliot's 'dissociation of sensibility', and to theories of 'the symbolic image' (with due acknowledgment of 'Mr. Frank Kermode's forthcoming book *Romantic Image*'). This is all very much to the point and symptomatic of critical concerns at the time—particularly at Reading—but what makes the talk unmistakably Fletcher and no-one else, is the intimacy with its leading characters: 'Did Pater really know what his own image of Leonardo's image portended, or would he have raised his bristly eyebrows when he read Yeats's preface? I do not think there would have been a flicker.'

Those 'bristly eyebrows' bring Pater into the room. The same sense of supernatural manifestation occurs elsewhere when Fletcher reworks Yeats's mythologizing: 'Henley, the paralyzed viking; Johnson, the suave ambiguous Hellenistic head over the figurine body tapering away to vanishing-point; the uneasily bewigged Davidson; suggesting verdicts on life and art' (*WBYC*,

p. 141). For Fletcher, as for Yeats, 'people tend to be arrested in moments that reveal "a fragment of the divine life", an instant which has the effect of a complete statement, both stylized and spontaneous' (*WBYC*, p. 132). Correspondingly, the critic's encounters with the poet are neither parasitic nor opportunistic. They're appreciative, respectful and very mildly parodic. Like Yeats, Fletcher is a scene-maker, and the undercutting of self that he notes in the master is amplified, almost—though not quite—to the point of burlesque; he would sometimes refer to Johnson, Dowson, Beardsley and the rest as his own 'circus animals.'

By the 1980s, Fletcher, as one of the foremost international experts on the period, was being asked to compile anthologies of late nineteenth-century literature. He seized upon these invitations as chances to indulge his own tastes, which seemed more idiosyncratic at the time than they might do now. Individual authors are compressed into a single phrase. A Gissing novel sends 'a sour and authentic imaginative report' (*BPP*, xvii) on the state of the East End; Housman's atheism 'like his occasional Manichaeism, is ironic and impatient' (*BPP*, xlv). The late introductions also betray an awareness of recent developments in areas with which Fletcher was not personally much concerned, such as the sociology of the novel, and they frequently conclude with wry observations about the contemporary cultural milieu. There are surprises nonetheless. Despite the end of Empire and its literature, 'we must hope for a renewal from the old Commonwealth, from British Indians, British West Indians' (*BPP*, l). The reluctant soldier who had once been concerned about the injustice inflicted by the British empire upon its passive and colonised members now looked to their post-colonial descendants for literary leadership.

In Fletcher's scheme of things, history and poetry always interact with one another. Here he is visiting Lissadell, site of Yeats's great poem about the Gore-Booth sisters:

> Yet as one stands there it is not anticlimax that one feels: only the generous emotions remain. One can only murmur "mana! mana!", that power over the living that belongs to non-human objects and the dead. We stand on haunted ground, ground where objects are spiritually

> active: the dead are vivid here. It is not elegiac pause
> over the end of the Ascendancy way of life, or the
> history of the Gore-Booth family. It is that art has
> affected life; that history as Yeats intended has been
> stylized. The ghosts with whom Yeats conversed have
> indeed arisen and have here a permanent habitation,
> here and not in Manchester or on Stephens Green; here
> and in Yeats's poem. (*WBYC*, pp. 217–8)

Retracing footsteps, succumbing to 'mana', communing with the past, was rarely without irreverence. Among my favourites, one of many memorable journeys in time and space, is Fletcher's account of the funeral of Lionel Johnson in 1902 that he included in his remarkable edition of Johnson's *Collected Poems* (Revised ed., New York: Garland, 1982, p. xv), reimagined during a visit to a North London cemetery long after the event. The passage connects the suburban Londoner with the lover of buildings, the meditative impressionist with the conscious stylist who never missed a verbal chance.

> St. Mary's Catholic cemetery at Kensal Green is one of
> the bleakest of its class: its north side, sliced away by a
> railway cutting; on its south side, a rubbish dump, a
> dead canal, another railroad track; on the eastern flank,
> an older, Protestant counterpart with vaults and
> pyramids softened by frequent foliage; on the west, an
> escarpment of factory walls, some derelict, one
> manufacturing piston rings, another producing cocoa.
> The dead are humped together; the short sour grass
> crawls between graves. The space is seared with wind;
> there are virtually no trees....

It might easily seem like the morbid musings of a lone pilgrim—until, that is, the very last sentence, which invites us to join him, chortling at the passage of time.

> The grave stands in an older part of the cemetery, one
> rarely visited by its custodians, without offering of
> flowers. Its blight, its solitariness, its windy bareness are

appropriate, approximating somehow to those desolate spaces that haunted Johnson's verse, though mitigated by warm gusts of cocoa from the factory to the windward.

— John Stokes

THE PUBLICATIONS OF IAN FLETCHER

1935

*'Renunciation.' *Alleynian* (October 1935), 307. Signed 'Altair.'

1936

*'December—A Poem.' *The Anvil: Evening Literary Department of Goldsmith's College*, 1, no. 4 (December 1936), 95.

1937

*'Litany 4'; 'Ego sum via, et veritas, et vita'; 'Crucifixion'. *The Anvil: Evening Literary Department of Goldsmith's College*, 2, no. 6 (December 1937), 137, 146.

1938

*'The Elephants. From the French of Leconte de Lisle'; 'Poem: XVIII.' *The Anvil: Evening Literary Department of Goldsmith's College*, 2, no. 7 (March 1938), 176, 181.

*'Two Poems For September 1938 (1)'; 'Song For the Disciples Before The Resurrection.' *The Anvil: Evening Literary Department of Goldsmith's College*, 2, no. 8 (December 1938), 201, 221.

1940

*'Dictator.' *New Vision*, no. 7 (Autumn 1940), 6.

1941

*'December 25th.' *New Vision*, no. 8 (Winter 1940–41), 1.

*'Spiritual Sonnet.' *New Vision*, no. 9 (Spring 1941), 2.

*'Ode.' *New Vision*, no. 12 (Winter 1941–42), 2.

1942

**A Satire on the Rise of Learning in the dark Sudan.* Khartoum: privately published, 1942. Reproduced from typescript. Pp. 12.

**The Principles of Perversion and Disgrace. Testament of My Political Man. To the Insipid Homosexuals of Cambridge.* Khartoum: privately published, 1942. Reproduced from typescript. Pp. 8.

*'A Love Song of Peter Abailard.' *Poetry Quarterly*, 4 (Summer, 1942), 51–52.

*'Love Poem.' *Poetry Quarterly*, 4 (Winter, 1942), 145. Reprinted in Keidrich Rhys, ed., *More Poems from the Forces* (London: Routledge, 1943), p. 89.

*'Coming to Cragmire.' *New Vision*, no. 13 (Spring, 1942), 3.

*'Poem.' *New Vision*, no. 14 (Summer, 1942), 13.

1943

A Passion Play. Khartoum: The Sudan Bookstore, 1943. Pp. 38.

*'When It Is Finished.' Denys Val Baker, ed., *Little Reviews Anthology*. London: Allen & Unwin, 1943, p. 175.

*'Dark Fires of Home.' *Poetry Review*, 34 (1943), 234. Reprinted as 'XLV' in *Poetry London*, X (1944), 52.

*'The Pattern and the Moment.' *Poetry Review*, 34 (1943), 292. Reprinted with minor revisions in *Orisons…* (1947), p. 70.

1944

*'Metaphysical Ode to General Lord Rawlinson in Heaven.' *Poetry London*, X (1944), 50.

*'Given With His Picture.' *Poetry London*, X (1944), 51.

*'Metaphysical Poem on a Cricket Match.' *Poetry London*, X (1944), 51.

*'A Poem of Blue Arches.' *Poetry London*, X (1944), 52.

*'XLV.' *Poetry London*, X (1944), 52. Previously appeared as 'Dark Fires of Home', *Poetry Review*, 34 (1943), 234.

*'XV: From Poems of the Real Presences. What was That?' *Poetry London*, 2, no. X (1944), 53.

'The Relationship Between Literature and Propaganda.' *Poetry London*, 2, no. X, (1944), 208–12.

*'Night-Fear (A Diptych).' *Poetry Quarterly*, 6 (Spring 1944), 6–7. Reprinted in *Orisons*… (1947), p. 15.

*'For my Cousin Lorna, God Keep Her'; 'Birthday Sonnet for K. M. F.' *Poetry Quarterly*, 6 (Summer 1944), 48. Reprinted in *Orisons*… (1947), pp. 73–74 and p. 74.

*'Unfruitful Hero.' *Dint* (Autumn 1944), 9.

Review of Charles Williams, *All Hallows Eve*. *Tripoli Times*, 14 October 1944. (Seen only as cutting.)

1945

**An Homily to Kenneth Topley Esq*. *Tripoli:* Privately printed, 1945. Pp. 8. (The British Library copy has extensive manuscript additions in Fletcher's hand.)

Several Praedications Ontologicall, Metaphisicall, Ineffectuall, Magastromantic and Holie. This item is typeset with the imprint: 'Made by Mr Saviour Billecci for the authour [*sic*] at the sign of the dancing Cherub in Costantine his street Tripoli of Barbarie, in th'imposthumous yeare of our salvation'; the date 'LDCCCCCLV' is added in ink. The text comprises 4 pp. There is a note on the title page in Fletcher's hand '2 copies only in existence. I. F.' (Seen only as pdf of the copy in Special Collections, Kenneth Spencer Research Library, University of Kansas, Lawrence, Kansas.)

*'Tano III.' *Poetry Quarterly*, 7 (Spring 1945), 16–17.

*'Hymn'; 'Sonnet.' *Poetry Quarterly*, 7 (Winter 1945), 125.

*'Parable.' *Outposts,* 5 (1945), not paginated.

'The Power of Conrad.' *Tripoli Times*, 18 November 1945, p. 2. Review of *Twixt Land and Sea.*

'Books. "The Great Gatsby".' *Tripoli Times*, 25 November 1945, p. 3.

'Ezra in the Pound.' *Tripoli Times*, 2 December 1945, p. 3.

'The Protestant Cemetery.' *Tripoli Times*, 9 December 1945, p. 3.

'Books. "The Colonel's Daughter" by Richard Aldington.' *Tripoli Times*, 9 December 1945, p. 3. Signed 'I. F.'

Review of 'The Polderoy Papers' by C. E. Vulliamy. *Tripoli Times*, 16 December 1945, p. 3.

'English Nativity Poetry.' *Tripoli Times*, 23 December 1945, p. 4.

*'Guide-Book to Tripoli.' *Tripoli Times*, 31 December 1945, p. 4.

'The Sulky City. A Dissident View of Tripoli.' *Tripoli Times*, 31 December 1945, p. 4.

1946

Epithalamia by various hands for the nuptials of George Sutherland Fraser and Eileen Lucy Andrew. London: Printed by Wyndham Printers Ltd. for Tambimuttu, 1946. [12] pp. + one unbound leaf. Unpaginated. Includes an untitled poem by Ian Fletcher, two quatrains, beginning: 'Gallons of Latin logic | Th'Aberdonian sturgeon drown'.

*'Sonnet'; 'Visitation.' *Poetry Quarterly*, 8 (Autumn 1946), 142.

1947

*Orisons picaresque and metaphysical. London: Editions Poetry, 1947. Pp. 74.

*[Untitled poem of forty-eight lines, beginning: 'Helen you who once have been.'] *Hymenaia: A Posie of Verse. Collected from Far & Wide To the Honour of John Conran Irwin, Asst. Keeper of the Indian Section, Victoria and Albert Museum and Helen Hermione Scott, one of the members of the House of Poetry.* London: Printed at Eversholt Printing Works, 1947. 16 pp, not paginated. Contains untitled poems by various hands.

*'Twin Poems on the Single Theme (T. T.)'; 'Metro-Delphic.' *Poetry London*, no. 12 (November-December 1947), 11–12. 'Twin Poems on the Single Theme (T. T.)' reprinted in *Motets* (1962), no. XII.

*'Chorus from a Not-to-be written Drama.' *Poetry Quarterly*, 9 (Autumn 1947), 138–39.

'Parthenia Sacra.' *TLS*, 15 November 1947, 591. Letter.

1948

*'Hélène.' *Poetry Review*, 39 (1948), 319.

*'A Marriage of Fountains.' *Poetry Review*, 39 (1948), 403.

*'Another Country'; 'Sonnet'; 'Sonnet.' *Poetry Quarterly*, 10 (Winter 1948), 212–13.

1949–1951

Nine (October 1949–April 1956). Iain Fletcher is listed as a member of the Editorial Board for the issues between October 1949 and Autumn 1951.

1949

*'Battista Guarini: Sogno della sua Donna. Translated by I.F.' *Nine*, I, no. 1 (October 1949), 10.

*'Girls at the Youth Centre.' *Nine*, I, no. 1 (October 1949), 13–14. Reprinted in revised form as 'Young girls in flower at the youth centre' in *Motets* (1962), no. XX.

*'Villanelle'; 'A Photograph of Ann.' *Poetry London*, 4, no. 15 (May 1949), 12–14.

*'Father and Son.' *Poetry London*, 4, no. 16 (September 1949), 10.

*'The Vision.' *Poetry Review*, 4, no. 16 (1949), 182–83.

*'Here To-Day.' *Forum: Stories and Poems*, 1.2 (1949), 40–41.

*'The Birth of Apollonius: a poem.' *The Occult Observer*, 1, no. 3 (1949), 189.

Review of George Woodcock, *The Incomparable Aphra*. *Poetry Review*, 40 (1949), 61.

Review of Henry Savage, ed., *The Love Letters of Henry VIII*; S. J. Looker, ed., *Elizabeth Barrett Browning, Selected Poems*; John Heath Stubbs, ed., *P. B. Shelley, Selected Poems*; Ruthven Todd, ed., *Selected Poems of William Blake*; Fred Marnau, ed., *Selected Poems of Christopher Marlowe*; Fred Marnau, ed., *Selected Poems of*

Andrew Marvell; Ronald Duncan, ed., *Rochester, Selected Lyrics and Satires*. *Poetry Review*, 40 (1949), 215–17.

'Ezra Pound.' *New Statesman*, 17 September 1949, 302. Letter.

1950

Introduction. *Parthenia Sacra*. Aldington: Hand and Flower Press, 1950. Pp. xxiv, 286.

*'Alonso de Ledesma's A la Lancadade, translated by Iain Fletcher.' *Nine*, II, no. I (January 1950), 28–29.

*'Mary the Dancer.' *Nine*, II, no. I (January 1950), 47. Reprinted in Robert Conquest, Michael Hamburger & Howard Sergeant, eds, *New Poems 1953: A P.E.N. Anthology*. London: Michael Joseph, 1953, pp. 92–3 and in *Motets* (1962), no. XVII.

*'An Ode Varient Upon Lord Herbert's *Iesus Patibilis*.' *Poetry London*, no. 18 (May 1950), 12–16.

'Adolescents in the Dusk.' reprinted in Anne Ridler, ed., *The Faber Book of Modern Verse*, rev. ed. London: Faber, 1951, p. 418.

'Stopping the Rot—II.' *Nine*, II, no. I (January 1950), 50–51.

'Editorial.' *Nine*, II, no. II (May 1950), 77.

*'Maurice Scève, Délie CCCLXXVIII [translated by Iain Fletcher with commentary]' *Nine*, II, no. III (August 1950), 203–05.

'The Fair Circassian.' *Nine*, II, no. IV (November 1950), 282–91.

'Four Unpublished Poems of Lionel Johnson. Edited by Iain Fletcher.' *Nine*, II, no. IV (November 1950), 328–30.

*'The Descent of the Word.' *Nine*, II, no. IV (November 1950), 335.

*'A Manual of Noumenal Beasts.' *Nine*, III, no. I (December 1950), 43–45. (with Peter Kneebone).

*'From a Sequence to Easter (v).' *Poetry Review*, 41 (1950), 68–69.

*'Here Today.' *Forum: stories and poems*, 1, no. 2 [1950], 40–41.

'Seven new Poems by Lionel Johnson. Selected by Iain Fletcher.' *Poetry Review*, 41 (1950), 315–18.

'John Skelton.' Review of H. L. R. Edwards, *Skelton*; Philip Henderson, ed., *The Complete Poems of John Skelton*. *New Statesman*, 21 January 1950, 72, 74.

'Poetry, Religion and Baroque.' Review of M. M. Mahood, *Poetry and Humanism*. *New Statesman*, 29 April 1950, 494.

'A Don's Dryden.' Review of David Nichol Smith, *John Dryden*. *New Statesman*, 3 June 1950, 635–36.

'Victorian Poetry.' Review of John Heath-Stubbs, *The Darkling Plain*. *New Statesman*, 15 August 1950, 211–12.

'The Wintry Paradox.' Review of Edith Sitwell, compiler, *A Book of the Winter*. *New Statesman*, 2 December 1950, 556.

'A Dictionary of Emblemata.' Review of Mario Praz, *Studies in Seventeenth-Century Imagery*. *Nine*, Vol II, no. I (January 1950), 56–58.

Review of Kathleen Raine, *The Pythoness*. *Nine*, II, no. II (May 1950), 147–48.

'Mad Logic.' Review of Christopher Smart, *Collected Poems*, ed. Norman Callan. *Nine*, II, no. III (August 1950), 247–49.

'A Revaluation of Some Victorian Poets.' Review of John Heath-Stubbs & David Wright, eds, *The Forsaken Garden*. *Nine*, II, no. III (August 1950), 249–51.

Review of M. P. Shiel, *Science, Life and Literature*. *Nine*, II, no. III (August 1950), 251. Signed 'I. F.'

Review of *Poetry London*, no. 17 (January 1950); *Poetry Quarterly* (Spring 1950); *The Glass*, no. 3; *Poetry Ireland* (April 1950). *Nine*, II, no. III (August 1950), 262.

'Sackville and the Rhetorical Tradition.' Review of J. Swart, *Thomas Sackville*. *Nine*, II, no. IV (November 1950), 337–39.

Review of Sylvia Fox-Strangways, *Poems*. *Nine*, II, no. IV (November 1950), 351.

'Current Periodicals.' Review of *TLS*, 25 August 1950. *Nine*, II, no. IV (November 1950), 353–54.

Review of *The Occult Observer*. *Nine*, II, no. IV (November 1950), 356.

Review of J. D. Hayward, ed., *The Penguin Donne*. *Nine*, III, no. I (December 1950), 74. Signed 'I. F.'

'A Modish Experience.' Review of Geoffrey Grigson, *The Victorians*. *Nine*, III, no. I (December 1950), 75–76.

'Moral Clarity at the Gala.' Review of Nicholas Moore, *Recollections of the Gala*. *Nine*, III, no. I (December 1950), 80–81.

'Current Periodicals.' Review of *Scrutiny*, 17, no. 2. *Nine*, III, no. I (December 1950), 88–89. Signed 'I. F.'

Review of Philip Henderson, ed., *The Complete Poems of John Skelton*; Roland Gant, selected and ed., *Poems by John Skelton*. *Poetry Review*, 41 (1950), 34–35.

Review of Nevill Coghill, *The Poet Chaucer*; Nevill Coghill, *Visions from Piers Plowman*; Ronald Duncan, ed., *Selected Poems of Ben Jonson*; Jack Lindsay, ed., *Selected Poems of William Morris*. *Poetry Review*, 41 (1950), 155–57.

Review of Peter Quennell, *The Pleasures of Pope; Poems of Alfred Lord Tennyson*; Norman Nicholson, *William Wordsworth*; F. S. Boas, ed., *Songs and Lyrics from the English Masques and Light Operas*; Kenneth Muir, ed., *The Collected Poems of Sir Thomas Wyatt*; R. N. Currey, *Formal Spring*; Geoffrey Grigson, ed., *Poems of John Clare's Madness*. Poetry Review, 41 (1950), 338–40.

1951

'The Role of Simonetta in Poliziano's *La Giostra*.' *Nine*, III, no. II (Autumn 1951), 109–12.

*'Angelo Poliziano (1454–1494) Simonetta.' *Nine*, III, no. II (Autumn 1951), 112–13.

'From Tasso to Marino.' *Nine*, III, no. II (Autumn 1951), 129–38.

'A Note on Gongora's *Poliferno*.' *Nine*, III, no. II (Autumn 1951), 188–90. Signed 'C. R.' *and* 'I. F.' (with D. S. Carne-Ross).

*'The Maenad Under the Cross.' *The Adelphi*, 27 (1951), 256.

*'Ad matrem: MCMXLV.' *Poetry Review*, 42 (1951), 76–77.

*'The Crucifixion of Simon the Cyrenian.' *Poetry London*, no. 22 (Summer 1951), 25.

'The Baroque Courtier.' *Nine*, III, no. II (Autumn 1951), 193–94. Review of David Mathew, *Sir Tobie Mathew*. Signed 'I. F.'

'The Poet as a Moral Agent.' Review of Samuel Daniel, *Poems and a Defence of Ryme*. *Nine*, III, no. II (Autumn 1951), 194–96.

Review of Richard Aldington, Introduction, *The Religion of Beauty. Selections from the Aesthetes*. Poetry Review, 42 (1951), 38–39.

Review of John Gawsworth (selected by), *The Poetical Works of Tennyson*. Poetry Review, 42, (1951), 352–53.

1952

Colonnade (Spring & Winter). Edited by Iain Fletcher, Ian Scott-Kilvert, D. S. Carne-Ross. Only two issues published separately; subsequently incorporated into *Adam International Review*.

*'Inest Deus Patiens.' *Colonnade*, no. 1 (Spring 1952), 13.

*'Dilectus meus candidus.' *Poetry Review*, 43 (1952), 80.

Review of Artura Barea, *Unanumo*; Cecil Spriggs, *Benedetto Croce*; Elizabeth Sewell, *Paul Valéry*; L. S. Salzberger, *Hölderlin*. *Colonnade*, no. 2 (Winter 1952), 52.

'To Win You Heaven.' Review of A. C. Southern, *English Recusant Prose*. *Nine*, III, no. 3 (April 1952), 282–87.

'Precursors of Yeats.' Review of Geoffrey Taylor, ed., *Irish Poetry of the Nineteenth Century*. *Nine*, III, no. 3 (April 1952), 291.

'The Metaphysics.' Review of Ruth Wallerstein, *Studies in Seventeenth Century Poetry*. *Nine*, III, no. IV (Summer Autumn 1952), 373–75.

'Blooms for Blimps.' Review of *Poems for Today, Fourth Series*. *Nine*, III, no. IV (Summer Autumn 1952), 379.

Review of F. Pratt Green, *The Unlikely Earth*; Gwynneth Anderson, *A Time to Speak*; Thomas Blackburn, *The Outer Darkness*; John Alden, *The Crossways*; John O'Hare, *The Return*. *Poetry Review*, 43 (1952), 167–68.

'Anthology of Younger Poets.' *TLS*, 21 November 1952, 761. Letter. (with G. S. Fraser)

'Younger Poets.' *The Spectator*, 24 October 1952, 538. Letter. (with G. S. Fraser)

'Younger Poets.' *New Statesman*, 1 November 1952, 512. Letter. (with G. S. Fraser)

1953

Ed., *The Complete Poems of Lionel Johnson*. London: Unicorn Press, 1953. Pp. xlv, 395. Revised ed., *The Collected Poems of Lionel Johnson*. New York: Garland, 1982.

Ed. and introduced, with G. S. Fraser. *Springtime: An Anthology of Young Poets and Writers*. London: Peter Owen, 1953.

*'Villanelle.' *The Listener*, 6 August 1953, 216.

*'In Veritatem ex Umbris Transiens.' *Poetry Quarterly*, 15 (Spring–Summer 1953), 10–13.

*'To Adam.' *Adam International Review*, no. 234 (1953), 12. (with G. S. Fraser)

*'The Hippolytus of Euripides. A New Version of 1–176.' *Adam International Review*, nos 235–236–237 (1953), 15–48. (with D. S. Carne-Ross). This is also *Colonnade*, II, no. 4 (Autumn 1953). Reprinted in John D. Yohannan, ed., *Joseph and Potiphar's Wife in World Literature: An Anthology of the Chaste Wife and the Lustful Stepmother*, New York: New Directions, 1968, pp. 28–77.

'"Colonnade" and Mr Fraser.' *The Spectator*, 18 September 1953, 300. Letter.

'Poetic Criticism.' *The Spectator*, 2 October 1953, 352. Letter.

1954

*'Angelo Poliziano, La Giostra *Simonetta*, I: 43–44, 47.' L. R. Lind, ed., *Lyric Poetry of the Renaissance with verse translations*. London: Oxford University Press, 1954, pp. 249–54.

*'Country of Masks'; 'Lynn Regis.' *Listen*, 1, no. 3 (Winter 1954), 14–15. 'Lynn Regis' reprinted in *Motets* (1962), no. I.

*'Orphica Luna.' *Chanticleer*, 1, no. 4 (Spring 1954), 34.

*'Journal.' *Platform*, 3 (Winter 1953/54), 32–33. (Front cover dates this 'Spring 1954.') Reprinted in *Motets* (1962), no. XIII.

*'Christ Church, Spitalfields.' *TLS*, 14 May 1954, 307.

*'Baroque Organ in a Northern Church.' *Encounter* (June 1954), 32. Reprinted in *Motets* (1962), no. II.

'The Poetry of Robert Garioch.' *Chanticleer*, 1, no. 4 (Spring 1954), 35–37.

'The Dualist Tradition.' *TLS*, 3 September 1954, 557. Letter.

1955

'The Dark Angel.' *Interpretations*, ed. John Wain. London: Routledge, 1955, pp. 153–78. Reprinted in revised form in *WBYC*, pp. 303–40.

*'The Mutations of Eros.' *TLS*, 29 July 1955, 422. Reprinted in *Motets* (1962), no. IX.

*'Numen.' *Listen*, 1, no. 4 (Autumn 1955), 18.

1956

*'A Study in Time and Motion (J.E.B).' *Stand*, 11 (1956), 18–19. Reprinted as *"Time and Motion Study.' George Fraser, ed., *Poetry Now: An Anthology*. London: Faber & Faber, 1956, pp. 63–64.

*'Baroque Madonna.' Stephen Spender, Elizabeth Jennings & Danny Abse, eds, *New Poems, 1956: A P. E. N. Anthology*. London: Michael Joseph, 1956, pp. 77–78.

*'The Lovers Martyrdom: The Madrigals of Torquato Tasso.' *Adam International Review*, no. 252 (1956), 20–24. This is also *Colonnade*, II, no. 7 (Summer 1956).

1957

*The Lover's Martyrdom: Translations from the Italian of Dante, Guarini, Tasso and Marino with Original Texts. Swinford: Fantasy Press, 1957. Pp. 25.

I, the Poet William Yeats. A descriptive guide to the photographic exhibition illustrating the life and works of W. B. Yeats. [Issued in connection with an exhibition held in the University of Reading.] pp. ii, 32. Mimeographed. (with D. J. Gordon and the assistance of Frank Kermode and others.)

*'Mr Hawksmoor: The Embittered Roman.' Clifford Dyment, ed., *New Poems 1957*. London: Michael Joseph, pp. 48–49. Reprinted in *Motets* (1962), no. VI.

'Leda and St Anne.' *The Listener*, 21 February 1957, 305–07.

*'St Lawrence, Whitchurch.' *Tamesis* (Summer 1957), 10–11. Reprinted in *Motets* (1962), no. VIII.

'Classical Influences.' *TLS*, 5 April 1957, 210. Review of C. A. Trypanis, *The Stones of Troy*. Unsigned.

1958

*'Just Pot-Pourri From a Betjeman Slag Heap.' *Engagé* [Reading, 1958]; not paginated; reproduced from typescript. An unsigned poem titled 'Pot-Pourri From a Betjeman Slag-Heap' appeared in *Tamesis* (May 1966), 16. Reprinted in revised form in James Hogg, ed., *The Servant of the Muse. A Garland for Peter Russell on his Sixtieth Birthday*. Salzburg Studies in English Literature 65. Salzburg: Institut für Anglistik und Americanistik, 1981, pp. 161–64.

*'The Nightingale.' *Tamesis* (1958), 18. Reprinted in *Motets* (1962), no. XVI.

'Two Poems by Rolfe.' *TLS*, 12 December 1958, 721. Letter.

1959

Walter Pater. London: Longmans, Green, 1959. Pp. 44. Revised ed. 1971. Reprinted in Ian Scott-Kilvert, general editor, *British Writers*, Volume 5. New York: Charles Scribner's Sons, 1982, and in Harold Bloom, ed., *Modern Critical Views of Walter Pater*, New York: Chelsea House Publishers, 1985, pp. 41–73.

*'Four Epigrams from the Greek Anthology'; 'A Comico-Chiliastic Evening's Entertainment.' *Tamesis* [1959], 30–31, 39.

'Elizabethan Sonneteer.' *TLS*, 10 April 1959, 210. Review of *The Poems of William Alabaster*, ed. G. M. Story & Helen Gardner. Unsigned.

'Critic of the Nineties.' *TLS*, 14 August 1959, 473. Review of Vincent O'Sullivan, *Opinions*. Unsigned.

'Why Not Take Pater Seriously?' *Essays in Criticism*, 9 (1959), 411–18. Review of Edmund Chandler, *Pater on Style*.

Review of Peter Allt & Russell K. Alspach, eds, *The Variorum Edition of the Poems of W. B. Yeats. Victorian Studies*, 2 (1959), 72–75.

1960

'Explorations and Recoveries—II: Symons, Yeats and the Demonic Dance.' *London Magazine*, 7.6 (1960), 46–60. Reprinted in *WBYC*, pp. 252–66.

'The Lallans Poets.' *TLS*, 16 September 1960, 593. Letter.

'Purple Couplet.' *Sunday Times*, 18 September 1960, 12. (Letter identifying some lines from Alfred Austin.)

1961

W. B. Yeats: Images of a Poet. By D. J. Gordon, with
Contributions from Ian Fletcher, Frank Kermode and Robin
Skelton. Manchester: Manchester University Press, 1961.
Pp. 151. Reprinted 1970. One chapter, 'Byzantium,' reprinted
in John Unterecker, ed., *Yeats: A Collection of Critical Essays*
(Englewood Cliffs, N. J.: Prentice-Hall, 1963), pp. 131–38.

'The 1890's: A Lost Decade.' *Victorian Studies*, 4 (1961), 345–54.

'The Present State of Yeats Criticism.' *Literary Half-Yearly*, 2.2
(July 1961), 22–26.

*'The Bom Jesus Stairs at Braga.' *TLS*, 13 October 1961, 742.
Reprinted in *Motets* (1962), no. V.

*'Lynn Regis'; 'The Palazzo of the Sun (Ovid Met II).' *Tamesis*
(Spring 1961), 14–15. Reprinted in *Motets* (1962) as no. I and
no. IV.

'Metaphysical Poetry.' Review of Joseph E. Duncan *The Revival
of Metaphysical Poetry*. *Essays in Criticism*, 11 (1961), 203–10.

1962

**Motets: Twenty One Poems*. Reading: School of Fine Art,
University of Reading, 1962. Pp. 47. 150 copies printed.

'Le Symbolisme français en Angleterre.' *Revue de Littérature
Comparée*, 36 (1962), 158–59.

'Some Unpublished Letters of Ernest Dowson to Herbert
Horne.' *Notes and Queries,* n. s. 9 (1962), 100–05.

'A Scots Poet.' Review of Maurice Lindsay, ed., *John Davidson: A
Selection of his Poems*. *Essays in Criticism*, 12 (1962), 435–41.

'Libertine and Pilgrim.' Review of V. de Sola Pinto, *Enthusiast in Wit: A Portrait of John Wilmot, Earl of Rochester*. *The Listener*, 17 May 1962, 870–71.

1963

*'Aristophanes *Thesmophoriazusae.*' *Arion: A Quarterly Journal of Humanities and the Classics*, 2, no. 3 (Autumn, 1963), 78–85.

'The Poetry of John Gray.' *Two Friends: John Gray and André Raffalovich*, ed. Fr. Brocard Sewell. [Aylesford]: St. Albert's Press, 1963, pp. 50–69. Reprinted in revised form in *WBYC*, pp. 269–302.

'The Art of Translation and Christopher Logue's *Patrocleia.*' *View* [Wantage Hall, University of Reading] (June 1963), 6–9.

'The Beardsley Nineties.' *View* [Wantage Hall, University of Reading] (June 1963), 21–3. Signed 'L Gray Johnson.'

'Only a Magnifying Glass.' Review of Jon Stallworthy, *Between the Lines*, in *The Review*, 9 (1963), 53–58. (with D. J. Gordon).

Review of Germain D'Hangest, *Walter Pater: L'Homme et L'Oeuvre*. *MLR*, 58 (1963), 415–17.

Review of Alethea Hayter, *Mrs Browning*. *Critical Quarterly*, 5 (1963), 181–83.

Review of P. Faulkner, *William Morris and W. B. Yeats*. *MLR*, 58 (1963), 626.

Review of Mark Longaker ed. *The Poems of Ernest Dowson*. *The Listener*, 16 May 1963, 840.

Review of Rupert Croft-Cooke, *Bosie*. *The Listener*, 23 May 1963, 879.

Review of Roger Lhombreaud, *Arthur Symons: A Critical Biography*. *The Listener*, 20 June 1963, 1045.

Review of Aiden Reynolds & William Charlton, *Arthur Machen*. *The Listener*, 17 October 1963, 625.

'Knowing the Worst.' Review of George Macbeth, ed., *The Penguin Book of Sick Verse*. *The Listener*, 5 December 1963, 947.

1964

John Milton, Paradise Lost. Books I & II. *Notes on Literature*, no. 37 (August 1964). London: British Council. Pp. 12.

'Sir John Vanbrugh: the amateur as genius.' *The Listener*, 17 September 1964, 424–26.

Review of Mark Longaker, ed., *The Poems of Ernest Dowson*. *MLR*, 59 (1964), 122–23.

Review of H. Montgomery Hyde, *Oscar Wilde: The Aftermath*. *MLR*, 59 (1964), 284–85.

'John Addington Symonds.' *TLS*, 5 November 1964, 999. Letter.

1965

W. B. Yeats. A Centenary Exhibition. Reading: University Library, 1965. Checklist of items by Ian Fletcher. Reproduced from typescript. Pp. 10.

'Yeats and Lissadell.' D. E. S. Maxwell & S. B. Bushrui, eds, *W. B. Yeats, 1865–1965: Centenary Essays on the Art of W. B. Yeats*. Ibadan: Ibadan University Press, 1965, pp. 62–78. Reprinted in revised form in *WBYC*, pp. 197–219.

'Rhythm and Pattern in *Autobiographies*.' Denis Donoghue & J. R. Mulryne, eds, *An Honoured Guest: New Essays on W. B. Yeats*. London: Arnold, 1965, pp. 165–189. Reprinted in revised form in *WBYC*, pp. 127–52.

*'Ekphrasis: Lights in Santa Sophia, from Paul the Silentiary.' *Arion: A Quarterly Journal of Classical Culture*, 4, no. 4 (Winter, 1965), 563–64. Reprinted in D. S. Carne-Ross, *Classics and Translation* (Lewisburg, PA: Bucknell University Press, 2010), pp. 267–68.

*'John Lennon in his own wrote.' *Tamesis* (January 1965), 20.

Review of Rosalie Glynn Grylls, *Portrait of Rossetti*; Gale Pedrick, *Life with Rossetti*. *The Listener*, 28 January 1965, 157.

1966

'Some Anticipations of Imagism.' J. Howard Woolmer, *A Catalogue of the Imagist Poets*. New York: AMS Press, 1966, pp. 39–54.

*'In Honour of Dorian and his Creator.' Translation of Lionel Johnson, 'In Honorem Doriani Creatorisque Eius.' Karl Beckson, *Aesthetes and Decadents of the 1890s: an anthology of British poetry and verse*. New York: Vintage, 1966, p. 117.

Review of Peter Gunn, *Vernon Lee: Violet Paget, 1856–1935*; Phyllis Grosskurth, *John Addington Symonds: A Biography*. *MLR*, 61 (1966), 115–17.

Review of J. G. Riewald, ed., *Max in Verse: Rhymes and Parodies*; Rupert Hart-Davis, ed., Max Beerbohm, *Letters to Reggie Turner*; Lord David Cecil, *Max: A Biography*. *Victorian Studies*, 9 (1966), 276–79.

Review of Barbara Charlesworth, *Dark Passages: The Decadent Consciousness in Victorian Literature*. *MLR*, 61 (1966), 693–95.

Review of Peter Gunn, *Vernon Lee*. *Literaturnaya Rossiya*, 61 (1966), 115–17.

'Symons and Beardsley.' *TLS*, 18 August 1966, 743. Letter.

1967

Beaumont and Fletcher. London: Longmans, Green, 1967.
Reprinted in Ian Scott-Kilvert, general editor, *British Writers*,
Volume 2. New York: Charles Scribner's Sons, 1982.

Ed. *Romantic Mythologies*. London: Routledge, 1967. Pp. xiii, 297.
Includes 'Bedford Park: Aesthetes Elysium?', pp. 169–207;
reprinted in revised form in *WBYC*, pp. 43–82.

'A Note on the Reputation of Elkin Mathews.' J. A. Edwards &
Patricia Hutchins, *Elkin Mathews—Poet's Publisher (1851–1921)*.
Exhibition held in The Library of The University of Reading
during the month of May 1967. Reproduced from typewriting.
Not paginated.

'Types and Emblems in Victorian poetry.' *The Listener*, 25 May
1967, 679–81.

*'Times Lost.' *The Literary Half-Yearly*, 8 (1967), 3–6.

*'The Apotheosis of Old Father Time.' *Tamesis* (Summer 1967), 10.

'Pursuit and Loss.' Review of Desmond Flower, ed., *The Poetical
Works of Ernest Dowson*; Desmond Flower, ed. *The Letters of
Ernest Dowson. TLS*, 2 November 1967, 1034. Unsigned.

Review of John A. Cassidy, *Algernon Charles Swinburne. MLR*, 62
(1967), 515–16.

'Symons and Beardsley.' *TLS*, 12 January 1967, 27. Letter.

'War Wounds.' *TLS*, 28 September 1967, 888. Letter.

1968

The Milesian Intrusion: A Restoration Comedy Version of Iliad XIV.
Nottingham: Byron Press, 1968. Pp. 9.

'History and Vision in the Work of W. B. Yeats.' *Southern Review*, 4 (1968), 105–26.

'Amendments and Additions to *The Complete Poems of Lionel Johnson* (1953).' *Victorian Newsletter*, 33 (1968), 38–43.

'Genius Without Dossier.' *The Listener*, 4 July 1968, 8–11.

*'Loie Fuller Dancing.' *The Literary Half-Yearly*, 9.1 (1968), 3–5.

*'Epilogue, "On Certain Third Programme Productions of the Greek Tragic Poets".' *New Signature*, no. 2 (November 1968), 18.

Review of Robin Skelton and Ann Saddlemyer, eds, *The World of W. B. Yeats: Essays in Perspective*. MLR, 63 (1968), 228–29.

'Survivor.' Review of Ann Blainey, *The farthing poet: a biography of Richard Hengist Horne 1802–1884*. *New Statesman*, 12 April 1968, 484, 486.

'Pater's Pilgrimage.' Review of Gerald C. Monsman, *Pater's Portraits: Mythic Pattern in the Fiction of Walter Pater*. *TLS*, 18 April 1968, 398. Unsigned.

'The Little Magazine, IV: "The Savoy".' Review of reprint of *The Savoy, nos 1–8, 1896*. *TLS*, 25 April 1968, 431–32. Unsigned.

'Dowson Re-Done.' Review of Mark Longaker, *Ernest Dowson*. *TLS*, 20 June 1968, 636. Unsigned.

'Chaps Like Us All.' Review of Rupert Croft-Cooke, *Feasting with Panthers*. *TLS*, 20 June 1968, 636. Unsigned.

Review of Jacqueline Van Voris, *Constance Markiewicz in the Cause of Ireland*; Anne Marreco, *The Rebel Countess: The Life and Times of Constance Markiewicz*. *Victorian Studies*, 12 (1968), 111–13.

Review of Richard Murphy, *The Battle of Aughrim*. *New Signature*, no. 1 [1968], 3–6.

'Little Magazines.' *TLS*, 23 May 1968, 529. Letter.

1969

'Sad Inheritance.' Review of John Dixon Hunt, *The Pre-Raphaelite Imagination*. *New Statesman*, 10 January 1969, 50–51.

'Fictions and Monologues.' Review of George Macbeth, ed., *The Penguin Book of Victorian Verse*. *New Statesman*, 7 March 1969, 333–34.

'Restoration Paperweight.' Review of James Sutherland, *Oxford History of English Literature, Vol VI: English Literature of the Late Seventeenth Century*. *New Statesman*, 4 April 1969, 484–85.

'The Vulnerable Yeats.' Review of A. Norman Jeffares, *A Commentary on the Collected Poems of W. B. Yeats*; Jon Stallworthy, *Vision and Revision in Yeats's Last Poems*; Joseph Ronsley, *Yeats's Autobiography*; Liam Miller, ed., *The Dolmen Press Centenary Papers*. *New Statesman*, 27 June 1969, 918.

'Unwilling Dross.' Review of John G. Hayden, *The Romantic Reviewers 1802–1824*. *New Statesman*, 8 August 1969, 184.

'The Survival of Clough.' Review of David Williams, *Too Quick Despairer: The Life and Works of Arthur Hugh Clough*. *New Statesman*, 19 December 1969, 899.

Review of Jean C. Noël, *George Moore: L'homme et l'oeuvre (1852–1933)*. *MLR*, 64 (1969), 156–57.

Review of G. C. Monsman, *Pater's Portraits: Mythic Pattern in the Fiction of Walter Pater*. *Review of English Studies*, n. s. 20 (1969), 240–41.

1970

An Exhibition of Book Design, Chiefly British, 1855–1910. Devised by Ian Fletcher. Cyclostyled, ff. 34. Reading: [Reading University Library], 1970.

'Terence Tiller.' Rosalie Murphy & James Vince, eds, *Contemporary Poets of the English Language.* New York: St Martin's Press, 1970, pp. 1093–95.

'Herbert Horne: The Earlier Phase.' *English Miscellany*, 21 (1970), 117–57.

'Adelaide Crapsey's *Cinquains.*' *Adam International Review*, 35 (1970), 62–64.

*'Woman from Genoa.' *Ariel*, 1 (1970), 101.

'Furtive Aesthete.' Review of *Letters of Walter Pater*, ed. Lawrence Evans. *New Statesman*, 31 July 1970, 126–27.

Review of Herbert M. Schueller & Robert L. Peters, eds, *The Letters of John Addington Symonds, MLR*, 65 (1970), 405–06.

Review of G. Levine & W. Madden, eds, *The Art of Victorian Prose. Review of English Studies*, n. s. 22 (1970), 98–100.

1971

Ed. *Meredith Now: Some Critical Essays.* London: Routledge, 1971. Includes Fletcher's 'Preface,' pp. vii–xiii; '*The Shaving of Shagpat*: Meredith's Comic Apocalypse,' pp. 34–68. Pp xiv, 317.

'Poet and Designer: W. B. Yeats and Althea Gyles.' *Yeats Studies*, 1 (1971), 42–79. Reprinted in revised form in *WBYC*, pp. 166–96.

'Letters to Herbert Horne, Ernest Radford and Elkin Matthews.' *Yeats Studies*, 1 (1971), 203–38.

*'Voyage to Montevideo' (translation of Dino Campana, 'Viaggio a Montevideo')'; 'The Rescue' (translation of Daniel Moyano). *Southern Review*, 7 (1971), 902–05, 934.

'Can Haggard Ride Again?' *The Listener*, 29 July 1971, 136–38.

'French Symbolist painting: the other tradition.' *The Times*, 2 June 1972, p. 17.

Review of Patricia Merivale, *Pan the Goat God: His Myth in Modern Times*. *MLR*, 66 (1971), 173–74.

Review of Richard J. Finneran, ed*., William Butler Yeats: John Sherman and Dhoya. Notes and Queries*, n. s. 18 (1971), 275–76.

'Echo Images.' Review of C. K. Hyder, ed., *Swinburne: The Critical Heritage. TLS*, 16 July 1971, 836. Unsigned.

1972

Ed., with Introduction. *Selections from British Fiction, 1880–1900*. New York: New American Library, 1972. Pp. 432.

'The Ellis–Yeats–Blake Manuscript Cluster.' *The Book Collector*, 21 (1972), 72–94.

'Edwin Ellis's Letter to Fairfax Murray, 31 Jan. 1892.' *The Book Collector*, 21 (1972), 414.

'A Study in Black and White: The Legend and Letters of Beardsley.' Review of Henry Maas, J. J. Duncan & W. G. Good, eds, *The Letters of Aubrey Beardsley*; *The Lysistrata of Aristophanes*, translated by Samuel Smith, illustrated by Aubrey Beardsley. *TLS*, 14 January 1972, 25–28. Unsigned.

Review of Mary L. Lago & Karl Beckson, eds, *Max and Will: Beerbohm and William Rothenstein: Their Friendship in Letters. New Review*, 2, no. 19 (1972), 68–70.

1973

Swinburne. Harlow: Longman for the British Council, 1973. Pp. 66. Reprinted in Ian Scott-Kilvert, general editor, *British Writers*, Volume 5, New York: Charles Scribner's Sons, 1982.

'Book Design and the Total Book, 1850–1900.' *Journal of the Francis Thompson Society*, 3 (1973), 7–23.

Review of Flavia Alaya, *William Sharp—'Fiona Macleod', 1855–1905*. *Yearbook of English Studies*, 3 (1973), 324–25.

Review of James G. Nelson, *The Early Nineties: A View from the Bodley Head*. *Review of English Studies*, n. s. 24 (1973), 103–05.

'Yeats's Quest for Self-Transparency.' Review of Denis Donoghue, ed., W. B. Yeats, *Memoirs. Autobiography-First Draft*; Robert O'Driscoll & Lorna Reynolds, eds, *Yeats Studies*, vols. 1–2; Michael J. Sidnell, George P. Mayhew & David R. Clark, *Druid Craft: The Writing of the Shadow Waters*. *TLS*, 19 January 1973, 53–55. Unsigned. Reprinted in *WBYC*, pp. 153–65.

'The Beardsley Void.' Review of Malcolm Easton, *Aubrey and the Dying Lady: A Beardsley Riddle*. *TLS*, 9 February 1973, 143. Unsigned.

1974

Ed. with Introduction and notes. *The collected poems of Victor Plarr*. London: Eric & Joan Stevens, 1974. Pp. xvii, 172. 750 copies.

The Group: an exhibition of poetry, 17 June to 10 December 1974. Reading: Reading University Library, 1974. (with John Pilling). Pp. 54.

Introduction to and description of 'The archives of Elkin Mathews, 1811–1938.' *The Archives of British and American Publishers on Microfilm*. Cambridge: Chadwyck Healey, 1974.

'Beaumont and Fletcher.' *The New Encyclopædia Britannica*, 15th edition, Chicago, IL: Encyclopædia Britannica Inc., 1974, pp. 782–84. Signed 'I. Fl.'

'John Todhunter's Lectures on Blake, 1872–1874.' *Blake Newsletter: An Illustrated Quarterly*, 8 (1974), 4–14.

'The white rose rebudded: neo-Jacobitism in the 1890s.' *Journal of the Francis Thompson Society*, 4–5 (1974), 17–52. Reprinted in revised form in *WBYC*, pp. 83–123.

Review of Malcolm Brown, *The Politics of Irish Literature: From Thomas Davis to W. B. Yeats*; Karl Beckson, *Oscar Wilde: the critical heritage*. *Notes and Queries*, n. s. 21 (1974), 37–39.

Review of John Stokes. *Resistible Theatres, enterprise and experiment in the late nineteenth century*. *Review of English Studies*, n. s. 25 (1974), 362–65.

'Whiffs of Decadence.' Review of Philippe Jullian, *The Symbolists*. *TLS*, 15 February 1974, 161. Unsigned.

'With the Courage of its Modernness.' Review of reprint of *The Yellow Book*. *TLS*, 29 March 1974, 344. Unsigned.

1975

'The Life of Quintilius.' Peter Russell, *The Elegies of Quintilius*. London: Anvil Press Poetry, 1975, pp. xi–xii.

'The traffic in Yeats.' Review of William H. Pritchard, ed., *W.B. Yeats*. *TLS*, 2 May 1975, 490.

'Inside Mr Swinburne.' Review of Philip Henderson, *Swinburne*. *TLS*, 21 November 1975, 1380.

1976

'Oscar Wilde.' Richard J. Finneran, ed., *Recent Research on Anglo-Irish Writers*. New York: MLA, 1976, pp. 48–137. (with John Stokes)

*'Addio Chianni.' *TLS*, 2 January 1976, 15.

Review of Brocard Sewell, *Olive Custance: Her Life and Work*. *Journal of the Eighteen Nineties Society*, 6–7 (1975/6), 34–35.

1977

Ed., with John Stokes. *The decadent consciousness: a hidden archive of late Victorian literature: forty-two rare and important titles published in thirty-six volumes*. New York: Garland Publishing, 1977. A separately issued pamphlet, listing the contents of the series, includes the 'Editors' Introduction' (pp. 2–3).

Review of Dudley Young, *Out of Ireland: the poetry of W.B. Yeats*. *Journal of Beckett Studies*, 2 (Summer 1977), 105.

Review of Margaret Maison, *John Oliver Hobbes: Her Life and Work*; H. Montgomery Hyde, *Oscar Wilde. Journal of the Eighteen Nineties Society*, 8 (1977). 11–13.

1978

'The man behind the masks.' Review of Karl Beckson, *Henry Harland. TLS*, 1 December 1978, 1383.

'A Commendable Beginning: A Review Essay.' Review of Linda C. Dowling, *Aestheticism and Decadence. A Selective Annotated Bibliography. ELT*, 21 (1978), 198–202.

1979

Ed., with Malcolm Bradbury, David Palmer, *Decadence and the 1890s*. London: Arnold, 1979. Includes Fletcher, 'Decadence and the little magazines,' pp. 172–202. Pp. 216.

Ed., Lionel Johnson, *A letter to Edgar Jepson*. London: Eric & Joan Stevens, 1979. 175 numbered copies. Not paginated.

'Amendments and Additions to a Bibliography of John Gray.' *ELT,* 22 (1979) 62–67.

Review of Donald Erikson, *Oscar Wilde*. *Victorian Poetry*, 17 (1979), 278–81.

Review of Robert Langbaum, *The Mysteries of Identity: A Theme in Modern Literature*. *Victorian Poetry*, 17 (1979), 278–81.

Review of Roy Gasson, ed., *The Illustrated Oscar Wilde*; Sheridan Morley, *Oscar Wilde*; Louis Kronenberger, *Oscar Wilde*; J. E. Chamberlin & Alan Bird, *The Plays of Oscar Wilde*. *Victorian Studies*, 22 (1979), 487–91.

Review of The Chameleon. *Journal of the Eighteen Nineties Society*, 10 (1979), 15–16.

Review of Kenneth Clark, *The Best of Aubrey Beardsley*. *Journal of the Eighteen Nineties Society*, 10 (1979), 18–19.

1980

*Lauds: four poems. London: Eric & Joan Stevens, 1980. Not paginated.

*Continuities. Nottingham: Byron Press, [1980?]. Contains 'Edgar Allan Poe' (p. 11), 'Addio Chianni' (pp. 11–12), 'Cimitiera Protestante' (pp. 12–13), 'Ode to the University of Illinois at the Twin Cities of Urbana-Champaign' (pp. 14–15),

'I. M. Bernard Spencer' (pp. 15–16), 'Another Death in Venice' (pp. 16–17).

Victor Selwyn, Erik de Mauny, Ian Fletcher, G. S. Fraser, & John Waller, eds, *Return to Oasis: War Poems and Recollections from the Middle East 1940–1946*. London: Shepheard-Walwyn, 1980. Includes previously unpublished *'Soldiers at the Base', p. 157. Reprints (from *Orisons...*, 1947) *'Unquiet Lives at the Base'; *'Nones at the Cockshut Cabaret', the latter in heavily revised form and retitled 'Trooper Tufty Trotwell Sings at the Cockshot Cabaret,' pp. 90–91. Also includes Fletcher's essay 'War Anthologies,' pp. xxix–xxx. Pp. xxxiii, 254.

'Mimic Heavens: Milton's Century.' *Encounter* (July 1980), 69–78. Review of Roland Frye, *Milton's Imagery and the Visual Arts*; Louis Martz, *Poet of Exile: A Study of Milton's Poetry*.

Review of Richard Perceval Graves, *A. E. Housman, The Scholar Poet. Journal of the Eighteen Nineties Society*, 11 (1980), 15–16.

'G. S. Fraser.' *TLS,* July 4, 1980, 758. Letter. (with Paddy Fraser & John Lucas)

1981

White Light and Sand: An Exhibition of Poetry in the Middle East between 1939 and 1945. Devised by Ian Fletcher and Adrian Caesar. Reading: University of Reading Library, 1981. Ff. ix, 29. The 'Introduction', on ff. i–ix, is signed 'I. F.'

Ed., *Poems of G. S. Fraser*. Leicester: Leicester University Press, 1981. Pp. 208. (with John Lucas)

Ed. with an introductory note. John Barlas, *Six sonnets*. London: Eric & Joan Stevens, 1981. 95 numbered copies. Pp. 10.

*'An Octagon for Peter Russell: "Celia, Cecilia"; "Autumn Garden"; "The Tangy One"; "Bacchus and the Ice Maiden

Nicaea"; "Woman from Genoa"; "Pot Pourri from a Betjeman Slag Heap"; "Melusine"; "A Manichaean Demiurge Amuses Himself With an Apology".' James Hogg, ed., *The Servant of the Muse. A Garland for Peter Russell on his Sixtieth Birthday*. Salzburg Studies in English Literature 65. Salzburg: Institut für Anglistik und Americanistik, 1981, pp. 158–66.

'The wavering kind.' Review of Norman Alford, *The Rhymers' Club*. *TLS*, 14 August 1981, 939.

1982

Ed., with an Introduction and notes. George Gissing, *The paying guest*. Brighton: Harvester, 1982. Pp. xxxii, 172.

'"Leda and the Swan" as Iconic Poem.' *Yeats Annual*, 1 (1982), 82–113. Reprinted in revised form in *WBYC*, pp. 220–51.

'John Gawsworth: The Aesthetics of Failure.' *Malahat Review*, no. 63 (October 1982), 206–19.

1983

Ed. with John Stokes. *Degeneration and Regeneration: Texts of the Pre-Modern Era. A twenty-nine volume facsimile series representing the highly varied themes of the 1890s in fiction, prose and poetry*. New York: Garland, 1983. A separately issued pamphlet, listing the contents of the series, includes the 'Editors' Introduction'.

Ed. with a prefatory note. John Gray, *Five fugitive poems*. London: Eric & Joan Stevens, 1983. Not paginated.

Preface and Notes to Théodore de Banville, *The Kiss,* translated by John Gray. Edinburgh: Tragara Press, 1983. Pp. 21.

Victor Selwyn, Dan Davin, Erik de Mauny & Ian Fletcher, eds. *From Oasis into Italy: War Poems and Diaries from Africa and Italy 1940–1946*. London: Shepheard-Walwyn, 1983. This includes *'Friends Gone'; *'Naked Africa,' pp. 27–28. Pp. xxvi, 265.

'Oscar Wilde.' Richard J. Finneran, ed., *Recent Research on Anglo-Irish Writers*. New York: MLA, 1983, pp. 21–47. (with John Stokes)

Review of J. P. Houston, *French Symbolism and the Modernist movement: a study of poetic structures. Yeats. An Annual of Critical and Textual Studies*, 1 (1983), 198–202.

1984

'In way of introduction: *Marius* past and present.' *ELT*, 27 (1984) 5–10.

'A Rejoinder.' *ELT*, 27 (1984), 170–71.

'A Biography of T. Sturge Moore.' Review of Sylvia Sprigge, *Affectionate Cousins: T. Sturge Moore and Marie Appia*. *ELT*, 27 (1984), 256–58.

1985

*'Naked Africa'; 'Soldiers at the Base.' Victor Selwyn, Erik de Mauny, Ian Fletcher & Norman Morris, eds, *Poems of the Second World War*. London: Dent, 1985, pp. 76–77.

Review of Janet Egleson Dunleavy, ed., *George Moore in Perspective*. *Victorian Studies*, 28 (1985), 693–94.

'Ernest Rhys.' Review of J. Kimberley Roberts, *Ernest Rhys*. *ELT*, 28 (1985), 94–99.

'Dowson Letters.' Review of *New Letters from Ernest Dowson*, ed. with a Preface by Desmond Flower. *ELT*, 28 (1985), 323–24.

1987

Aubrey Beardsley. New York: Twayne, 1987. Pp. 206.

W.B. Yeats and his contemporaries. Brighton: Harvester, 1987. Pp. x, 350.

Ed., *British poetry and prose, 1870–1905.* Oxford: Oxford University Press, 1987. Pp. lvii, 497.

Ed., with notes. John Gray, *Some unpublished poems.* Edinburgh: Tragara, 1987. Pp. 37. 145 copies printed.

'A Grammar of Monsters: Beardsley's Obsessive Images and their Sources.' *ELT*, 30 (1987), 141–63.

'Some Aspects of Aestheticism.' O M Brack, ed., *Twilight of Dawn.* Tucson: Arizona State University Press, 1987, pp. 1–33. Reprinted in revised form in *WBYC*, pp. 3–42.

'The Dark Eminence of Modernism.' Review of Patricia Clements, *Baudelaire and the English Tradition. ELT*, 30 (1987), 81–85.

'Frederic Harrison.' Review of Martha S. Vogeler, *Frederic Harrison: Vocation of a Positivist. ELT*, 30 (1987), 362–65.

'Yeats: Letters and the Visual Arts.' Review of John Kelly, ed., *The Collected Letters of W. B. Yeats, Volume I 1865–1895. ELT*, 30 (1987), 475–81.

1988

Ed. *The poems of John Gray.* Greensboro, NC: ELT Press, 1988. Pp. xii, 359.

'Between Man and Beast.' Review of Bram Dijkstra, *Idols of Perversity: Fantasies of Feminine Evil in fin-de-siècle Culture. TLS*, 12 February 1988, 158.

'The in-between man.' Review of Wolfgang Iser, *Walter Pater;* William Buckler, *Walter Pater;* Paul Barolsky, *Walter Pater's*

Renaissance; R. M. Seiler, *Walter Pater*; Linda Dowling, *Language and Decadence in the Victorian Fin de Siècle*. *TLS*, 5 August 1988, 858.

'Sonny and the siren-slaves.' Review of Michael Holroyd, *Bernard Shaw: The Search for Love*. *TLS*, 16 September 1988, 1007–08.

'Ellmann's Oscar Wilde.' Review of Richard Ellmann, *Oscar Wilde*. *ELT*, 31 (1988), 309–12.

Review of Karl Beckson, *Arthur Symons: A Life*. *Victorian Poetry*, 26 (1988), 484–87.

Review of William H. O'Donnell, *The poetry of William Butler Yeats: an introduction*. *Yeats. An Annual of Critical and Textual Studies*, 6 (1988), 307–09.

1989

Victor Selwyn, Erik de Mauny, Ian Fletcher, & Robin Ivy, eds, *More Poems of the Second World War: The Oasis Selection*. London: Dent, 1989. Pp. xix, 383.

'Inventions for the Left Hand: Beardsley in Verse and Prose.' Robert Langenfeld, ed., *Reconsidering Aubrey Beardsley*. Ann Arbor: UMI Research Press, 1989, pp. 227–66.

Review of A Bookman's Catalogue: The Norman Colbeck Collection of Nineteenth-Century and Edwardian Poetry and Belles Lettres. *ELT*, 32 (1989), 223–26.

1990

Rediscovering Herbert Horne: Poet Architect, Typographer, Art Historian. Greensboro, NC: ELT Press, 1990. Pp. xv, 188.

Arthur Symons: A Bibliography. Greensboro, NC: ELT Press, 1990. Pp. xxi, 330. (with Karl Beckson, Lawrence W. Markert, John Stokes)

Essays & poems in memory of Ian Fletcher, 1920–1988. *ELT*, Special Series, Number 4 (1990). This includes the first printing of three poems: *'Cautionary Tale for Agnes' (pp. 158–59); *'For Genevra's Birthday' (pp. 162–64); *'A Ballad of the 1890's' (pp. 167–69).

1995

*'Egypt'; 'Christmas Letter Home.' *The Voice of War: Poems of the Second World War*. London: Michael Joseph for the Salamander Trust, pp. 38–39.

1998

Collected Poems. Introduction by Peter Porter. Nottingham: Shoestring Press, 1998. Pp. 146.

Broadcasts

These are all on the Third Programme or Radio 3. Repeats have not been included.

20 June 1955. 'The Girdle of Aphrodite.' A programme of new translations from ancient Greek love poetry. Selection and commentary by Ian Scott-Kilvert. Introduced by D. S. Carne-Ross. Versions by Edwin Morgan, Richard Murphy, Ian Scott-Kilvert, Constantine Trypanis, G. S. Fraser, Iain Fletcher.

10 July 1955. 'New Poetry.' Iain Fletcher introduces another programme of readings from recently published volumes of poetry.

17 July 1955. 'Tirsis and Cloris.' Iain Fletcher talks about Torquato Tasso as a writer of short lyrics.

8 August 1955. 'Poems from Byzantium.' A programme of new translations from Byzantine religious poetry by G. S. Fraser, Ian Scott-Kilvert, Iain Fletcher, Peter Green, Peter Levy, C. A. Trypanis.

17 September 1955. 'New Poetry.' Introduced by Iain Fletcher.

16 January 1957. 'Love's Duel.' A seventeenth-century dialogue for two voices. Arranged by Iain Fletcher.

26 January 1957. 'Leda and St Anne.' Published as 'Leda and St Anne,' *The Listener*, 21 February 1957, 305–07.

12 March 1957. 'Portrait of Ovid.' Written and narrated by Peter Green. Translations old and new by Henry Fielding, Arthur Golding, John Gower, Christopher Marlowe, Iain Fletcher, G. S. Fraser, Peter Green, Ian Scott-Kilvert.

14 December 1958. 'The Lament for Daphnis.' An enquiry into the pastoral tradition directed towards a reading of Milton's 'Lycidas' by John Gielgud. Translations by William

Arrowsmith, Edwin Morgan, Ian Scott-Kilvert, Iain Fletcher. Narrator: Iain Fletcher.

11 June 1959. 'Comment.' A weekly review of the arts. Including: Iain Fletcher on the Old Vic production of *The Tempest*, adapted from Shakespeare's play by Dryden and Davenant with music by Purcell—a new production to mark the tercentenary of Purcell's birth.

2 June 1960. 'Comment.' A weekly review of the arts. This edition includes Ian Fletcher on the Third Programme production of Etherege's *The Man of Mode*.

27 August 1960. 'The Mandolin' and 'Ipsissimus.' Two dramatic monologues by Eugene Lee-Hamilton (1845–1910). Introduced by Ian Fletcher.

13 October 1960. 'The Odyssey. Book X.' Translated by Ian Fletcher.

26 December 1960. 'The Corrupted Feast.' A literary miscellany of The Nineties compiled and introduced by Ian Fletcher with poems and prose passages from the works of John Davidson, Ernest Dowson, John Gray, Lionel Johnson, Theodore Julius Marzials, Amy Levy, Vincent O'Sullivan, Arthur Symons, John Addington Symonds, Sandys Watson, W. B. Yeats. Produced by George MacBeth.

17 February 1961. 'Jael.' A dramatic monologue by Lord De Tabley. Introduced by Ian Fletcher.

14 February 1962. 'New Comment.' A weekly review of the arts. Introduced by George MacBeth. This edition is devoted to Gilbert and Sullivan and includes Ian Fletcher on Gilbert's lyrics.

11 July 1962. 'New Comment.' A weekly review of the arts. This edition is devoted to The Chichester Theatre Festival and

includes Ian Fletcher on Sir Laurence Olivier's production of John Fletcher's comedy *The Chances*.

5 September 1962. 'New Comment.' This edition includes Ian Fletcher on *Patrocleia*, Christopher Logue's adaptation of the sixteenth book of the Iliad.

1 October 1962. 'Rite of Summer.' A personal view of cricket by Ian Fletcher.

2 July 1963. 'The Hippolytus of Euripides.' Translated by Ian Fletcher and D. S. Carne-Ross.

24 August 1964. 'The Amateur as Genius.' Ian Fletcher on Vanbrugh as dramatist and architect. Published as 'Sir John Vanbrugh: the amateur as genius,' *The Listener*, 17 September 1964, 424–26.

1 January 1965. 'A Festival of Women.' by Aristophanes in a version by Ian Fletcher.

15 August 1967. 'An Art of Pictures.' Printed as 'Types and Emblems in Victorian poetry.' Published in *The Listener*, 25 May 1967, 679–81.

25 February 1968. 'The Poetry of H. D.' Selected and introduced by Ian Fletcher.

9 April 1968. 'La Veneziana.' 'The Venetian Affair': an anonymous sixteenth-century comedy translated by Ian Fletcher and Luigi Meneghello.

9 June 1968. 'Genius Without Dossier.' A centenary talk by Ian Fletcher on the work of the Scottish architect and designer Charles Rennie Mackintosh 1868–1928.

28 December 1968. 'Renaissance Literature. Dante's "Inferno"' by Ian Fletcher.

5 June 1970. 'A Festival of Women by Aristophanes.' A transvestite comedy Radio 4. English version by Ian Fletcher.

28 June 1971. 'Rider Haggard'. Published as *'Can Haggard Ride Again?', The Listener*, 29 July 1971, 136–38.

10 June 1972. 'Arts Commentary.' Ian Fletcher, 'The Pre-Raphaelites and the Symbolists.'

Plays

'Get Up What Stairs.' Reviewed in *The Stage*, 29 April 1948, 4.

'A Mystery of the Passion.' Performed 4–8 April 1949, at the church of St. Thomas, Regent Street, London, with music by John Buckiand. Reviewed in *The Stage*, 7 April 1949, 7–8.

Recording

William Blake with illustrations read by Peter Orr, London: British Council Recorded Sound Section, 1972. Ian Fletcher describes Blake's life and discusses his early works, in particular *Songs of innocence* and *Songs of experience*.

APPENDIX: IAN FLETCHER'S LITERARY MANUSCRIPTS AND OTHER PAPERS

The largest collection of Ian Fletcher's papers is in Special Collections, University of Reading, Museum of Rural Life, MS 4619 1928–1984. We are grateful to Jennifer Glanville for information recorded below. The University of Reading online catalogue reports: 'the collection consists of poetry, articles, broadcast scripts, translations and notes by Ian Fletcher together with a large quantity of correspondence, some family papers and photographs of Ian Fletcher and his contemporaries.' Letters and other materials sent to Fletcher are catalogued separately.

[Boxes 1–3]

4619/1	Works by
4619/1/1	Poetry
4619/1/2	Other works

[Boxes 4–6]

[Box 4]

4619/2	Ian Fletcher as editor
4619/2/1	*Colonnade* literary magazine—correspondence
4619/2/2	*Nine* literary magazine—correspondence with IF and Peter Russell
4619/2/3	Salamander Oasis Trust anthologies [Boxes 4–6]

[Boxes 4–5]

4619/2/3/1	Letters and poems [mainly photocopies] by named individuals A–Z

[Box 5]

4619/2/3/2	Other poetry [mainly photocopies]

[Box 6]

4619/2/3/3	Periodicals [photocopies]

[Boxes 6–8]

4619/3	Other Correspondence—Alphabetical by correspondent, some including poems

[Box 8]

4619/4	Personal/family papers.
4619/4/1	Correspondence with family
4619/4/2	Photographs etc of Ian Fletcher and others

There are various manuscripts in the British Library. Additional MS 88907/7/8/3 includes some of Fletcher's literary manuscripts. Additional MS 88908/8/4/11 is his correspondence with Tambimuttu. Additional MS 89002/2/12 is his correspondence with Edward Upward.

Dulwich College Library has an exercise book, dated 1935, with the title 'Selected Poems by I. Fletcher.' This contains fifty-nine poems.

There are other Fletcher manuscripts in American university libraries, as follows:

The Kenneth Spencer Library, University of Kansas, Lawrence, Kansas:

MS 51D:I: '1940' folder, containing signed typescripts with some emendations for the poems "The Corn Lady" and "Agony of Dying Houses" (I, II, and [III?]).

MS 51D:II: '1943' folder, containing typescripts of approximately 58 poems, some with emendations/notes, many signed.

MS 51D:III: '1945' folder, containing proofs of poems by Fletcher, several signed by Fletcher to Gawsworth, or including corrections,: 'An Homily to Kenneth Topley ESQ.'; galley proofs of 'An Homily to Kenneth Topley ESQ.' proofs for 'Several Praedications,' includes the proof poems with emendations, 'Three Cerebral Pavanes, Untitled poem ('At the conjunction with the beautiful Hebrew Rina of fifteen years'), Untitled poem ('She sees the clouds like characters'), 'Exposition', 'Sonnet.'

MS 51D:IV: 39 pages of typescript and manuscript drafts of poems, with typed cover letter on University of Reading letterhead, dated 15th November, 1961 to 'The Secretary' at the University of Kansas.

MS 51D:V: "Letters" folder, containing correspondence from Fletcher to Charles Wrey Gardiner (two autograph letters signed, two typed letters signed, and two typed postcards signed, 1942–1953).

The Poetry Collection of the University Libraries, University at Buffalo, the State University of New York, Contemporary Manuscripts Collection, PCMS-0001):

Box 150 Folder 5: 'She's a hermaphrodite' in essence, since…' (AMs [1945?], 1 leaf)

Box 150 Folder 4: 'Three cerebral pauanes' (AMs [1945?], 2 leaves)

Box 150 Folder 4: 'Egypt' (TMs [1945?], 1 leaf)

Box 150 Folder 6: 'Dilectus meus candidus' (TMsS [1952?], 3 leaves)

(Box 150 Folder 7), an untitled manuscript (TMs, 1947, 47 pages total) with the following poems: 'Ekphrasis: Lights in Santa Sophia'; 'Lynn Regis'; 'Baroque Organ in a Northern Church'; 'St. Peter's (After D'Annunzio)'; 'Mr. Hawksmoor, the Embittered Roman'; 'Chapel of the Rotunda Lying-in-Hospital'; 'The Bom Jesus Stairs at Braqa'; 'The Palazzo of the Sun'; 'St. Lawrence: Whitchurch'; 'Great Pan is Dead'; 'Qui est Filius diceris et Pater inveniris'; 'The Mutations of Eros'; 'I am afraid of that…'; 'The Single Theme'; 'Journal'; 'A Villanelle at the Black and White Milk Bar'; 'The Poor Man's Audrey Hepburn'; 'Women Live by Remembrance'; 'Young Girls in Flower at the Youth Centre'; 'Mary the Dancer'; 'Loie Fuller'; 'The Nightingale'; 'A Chorus from Euripides'; 'Heraldic Mermaid, Melusine'; 'Doralice and Mandricardo'; 'Circe.'

Special Collections, Arizona State University Library, Tempe, AZ:

2015-04872 Fletcher, Ian Papers

The papers comprise six boxes that contain a wide range of notes, offprints, proofs and correspondence concerned with Fletcher's research interests. The last include materials relating to A. H. Mackmurdo, Elkin Matthews, John McBride, Sturge Moore, Max Nordau, Ezra Pound, Arthur Symons, Oscar Wilde and others. The papers also contain a bound volume relating to Selwyn Image.

In addition, there are several private collections to which we have had access.

THIS EDITION LIMITED TO 300 COPIES